Teaching Reading Fundamentals and Strategies with Social-Emotional Learning

Teaching Reading Fundamentals and Strategies with Social-Emotional Learning

Marjorie S. Schiering

ROWMAN & LITTLEFIELD
Lanham • Boulder • New York • London

Published by Rowman & Littlefield
An imprint of The Rowman & Littlefield Publishing Group, Inc.
4501 Forbes Boulevard, Suite 200, Lanham, Maryland 20706
www.rowman.com

86-90 Paul Street, London EC2A 4NE, United Kingdom

Copyright © 2024 by Marjorie S. Schiering

All rights reserved. No part of this book may be reproduced in any form or by any electronic or mechanical means, including information storage and retrieval systems, without written permission from the publisher, except by a reviewer who may quote passages in a review.

British Library Cataloguing in Publication Information Available

Library of Congress Cataloging-in-Publication Data

Names: Schiering, Marjorie S., 1943– author.
Title: Teaching reading fundamentals and strategies with social-emotional learning / Marjorie S. Schiering.
Description: Lanham, Maryland : Rowman & Littlefield, [2024] | Includes bibliographical references and index. | Summary: "This book provides six different strategies for teaching the fundamentals of reading with social-emotional learning in mind"— Provided by publisher.
Identifiers: LCCN 2023041373 (print) | LCCN 2023041374 (ebook) | ISBN 9781475868708 (cloth) | ISBN 9781475868715 (paperback) | ISBN 9781475868722 (epub) Subjects: LCSH: Reading. | Literacy. | Affective education. Classification: LCC LB1050 .S245 2024 (print) | LCC LB1050 (ebook) |
    DDC 418/.4071—dc23/eng/20230912
LC record available at https://lccn.loc.gov/2023041373
LC ebook record available at https://lccn.loc.gov/2023041374

Contents

Foreword   vii
Robert Kinpoitner

Preface   ix

Acknowledgments   xv

Introduction   xix

PART I: TEACHING READING FUNDAMENTALS   1

1. What Are You Thinking?   3
2. What Are You Feeling? Distinguishing Thinking from Feeling   13
3. Memory Definition with Examples and Three Types of Memory   17
4. Reading Involves Understanding = Comprehension   23
5. The Plot: Sequence of a Story   29
6. Character Counts with Social-Emotional Learning   31

PART II: TEACHING READING STRATEGIES PRELUDE   45

7. Guidelines: Oral Reading Presentations and Silent Reading Directives   47
8. Content of Chapters 9–14 with Explanations   53

PART III: TEACHING DIFFERENT READING STRATEGIES   61

9. The Reciprocal Reading Strategy   63

10	Orton–Gillingham Strategy *Catherine Colonna*	77
11	Reader's and Writer's Workshop *Natalie Simpson-White and Daniel Berger*	85
12	Shared Reading	103
13	Guided Reading *Joseph Aurilla, Danielle Bruno, and Alessia Giliberti*	113
14	Balanced Literacy's Independent Writing	123

PART IV: TEACHING READING THROUGH ANECDOTES AND SHORT STORIES — **131**

15	Anecdotes: Persons of Good Character	133
16	Short Stories	147

APPENDICES — **169**

Appendix A: Author's Closing Thoughts	171
Appendix B: Author's Poetry about Teaching	173
Bibliography	183
Index	187
About the Author and Contributors	193

Foreword

Once again, Professor Marjorie Schiering, EdD, tackles the challenging task of teaching reading to students in her latest book, *Teaching Reading Fundamentals and Strategies with Social-emotional Learning*. She melds the theoretical with the practical, but ever remains true to her concern that what she professes is positive and affirming to the students.

She begins carefully defining terms and delineating approaches to helping students understand what they read. Her years educating in grade school, middle school, college, and graduate settings helps translate these approaches to the realities teachers face. This is when working with all kinds of struggling youngsters. And so, she reminds these teachers, as they apply these methods, to respect their students, stress the positive, encourage, and care. They, both teacher and student, will then achieve their goals.

But this is not simply a philosophical text. Dr. Schiering quickly moves to a description of what takes place in the classroom. Everything from the setup of the room to the length of lessons is given consideration. And she illustrates her points with her own experiences teaching students in a variety of circumstances and in a variety of ways for those with difficulties and for those who need to be taught in a manner that addresses their processing preferences. In this instance she matches students' abilities with reading strategies.

The students are real; their learning circumstances are clear; Dr. Schiering's advice is sage; her results are evident. She invites her readers to face varied teaching strategies and intertwine that with activities to stimulate conversations. She invites teachers to enjoy the success of being a teacher and watch students achieve and to do so with kindness and consideration for a comfortable classroom environment where social and academic cognition are evident.

Dr. Schiering concludes her book with delightful stories she has gathered from colleagues and former students over the years. Their personal experiences make concrete points on several topics. Dr. Schiering shares about effective teaching of reading, as she connects these stories to the different reading strategies for use in a particular reading lesson. Still, she maintains the use of reading to stimulate thinking or to partake in it for the enjoyment of a story.

Professor Schiering's books, lectures, and presentations domestically and internationally have enriched her audiences with the joy of teaching reading. In this work, she continues guiding and praising those who accept the challenge of opening the printed page to the young. The pages are rich with scholarship and experience. The book is serious, smart, and detailed; provides a user-friendly read; and is skillfully written.

Robert Kinpoitner, PhD
Professor of English
School of Arts and Sciences
Molloy University

Preface

WHERE TO START?

Before addressing reading or its fundamentals, as two of the keywords in this book's title, this author thinks it's important to know exactly what teaching entails. Subsequently, that is the very first thing defined here, so you, as this book's reader, will be aware of what teaching involves and then, what encompasses learning.

Teaching: "This is the act of passing on information for the purpose of learning. Therefore, teaching may be accomplished in a variety of ways, and these are defined by the style of delivery or the way the material is presented" (Schiering et al., 2011). And there are three distinct styles known as the three D's: Directing, Discussing, and Delegating. The first of these promotes learning through listening and following directions. The second of the two promotes reading through interaction, and the third refers to the empowerment of learners. Perhaps Haugsbakk and Nordkvelle (2007) best explain teaching when they relate it to being "the facilitation of learning."

For teaching to be most effective and affective, the learner is understood to be more than a passive recipient of knowledge. Instead, the learner is one who is actively engaged in the learning process by being involved through the teacher's attention to students' needs. This is conducted on academic and social plains. Regardless, teaching impacts learning. So, you may wonder, what is that?

Learning: This is the process of linking comprehension to cognitive processes by developing skills that are genuinely transferable to everyday situations. "Learning is connected to reflective intelligence and affected by self-awareness, beliefs about one's abilities, clarity and strength of learning goals, personal expectations, and motivation to know about things" (Schiering, 2011; Abott, 1994). At its core learning involves memory, cognition, feelings/emotions, and touching on comprehension. Learning happens naturally without necessarily dwelling on what's occurring, but intrinsically realizing and recognizing information while comparing and contrasting what happens as well. However, more on that in chapter 1 of this book.

TEACHING READING

What do you suppose are the steps to be taken or to be experienced when teaching reading? Perhaps first you'll think students need to be able to "decode" words. This means they can have knowledge of letter-sound relationships, including letter patterns, and correctly pronounce written words. Granted, that is vital, as you're not going anywhere with teaching reading, or doing that for yourself without that ability in place.

Let's see, are you *thinking* of putting together words to form sentences for reading? And if so, you then realize that there are thoughts and *feelings* about what is being read. Sometimes, maybe most times, there's realizing and recalling the topic of what is being read. And, if this subject matter influenced you in some way. That would be labeled the use of *memory* to form opinions or responses to what has been read. Doing that remembering involves thinking or its synonym, cognition. Next would be comprehension of the material, whether in reading a story or information from a discipline-specific book in math, science, social studies, and so on. These terms in action of comprehension and reflecting or recalling which involve memory are the steps in going from the beginning to ending of a reading process.

Wait! With all this going on this author would be remiss in ignoring the book to be read or the story to be told. That has order as well. Simply stated, all of what you've read thus far could be addressed as "What you need for teaching reading." Please keep that in mind, as this Preface provides more information about teaching, learning, and reading.

HIERARCHY OF THE FUNDAMENTALS
FOR TEACHING READING

1. *Thinking/ Cognition.*
2. *Feelings.*
3. Use of one's *memory* to compare thinking and feeling from previous times to what's being read.
4. Realizing *comprehension* comes next with an understanding of what one reads to establish *meaning*. Comprehension = understanding, and understanding = comprehension.

5. Story *Plot*: Knowing the order and parts of a story or book.
6. *Character* and *Social-emotional Learning*, as these are continually interconnected when teaching is being modeled and learning is happening.

THE RECIPROCITY AND HIERARCHY OF TEACHING READING

In this preface, you have been introduced to the contents of this book with respect to teaching, learning, and the fundamentals of teaching reading. These have been presented in a *hierarchy* with memory and story plot, as well as comprehension with all involved in a sequence. Then too there is the social-emotional aspect of learning. And now these are being explained as involving the *reciprocal* mode. That italicized word simply means that the sequence shown with numbers 1–6 does not necessarily follow that pattern when teaching anything and that includes reading. No, the hierarchy was put there to establish what is involved in the fundamentals of teaching reading. The way these actually occur is oftentimes reciprocal.

So, why do you think that reciprocity may be important for the fundamentals of teaching reading? Well, it's mentioned due to being an integral part of one's basic awareness of what's involved in teaching this subject area. If you chose to widen your scope, then you'd likely discover the same or similar fundamentals for any subject matter that is presently taught in schools. They are offered in a hierarchy as a getting acquainted tool and offer a sense of security when seeing them placed in a particular order. However, within that hierarchy there is reciprocity. When you know the fundamentals, then you have the baseline for teaching with the style of delivery also taking a role. However, more on that later.

Perhaps a good synonym for things being reciprocal as opposed to in a structured hierarchy would be "simultaneous" presentation of material. While there is an order to be noted, so too is there an exchange within and between fundamental processes to be realized. Is there a thought before a feeling, or does a feeling trigger a thought? Is a thought stimulated by memory or some earlier comprehension, or is the material presented new to you—the reader. Do these skills happen within seconds of one another so that it is difficult to discern which came first? Yes, which comes first is likely difficult to discern for any cognitive or emotional experience.

This book has put the fundamentals of reading in sequential order for the sake of clearly defining each one in forthcoming chapters. In fact, these skills of thinking, feeling, memory, and comprehension are intertwined. They are interconnected and, in many situations, interdependent on one another. For what you may question and that would be for gaining meaning, which also encompasses definition, explanation, interpretation, or understanding.

SOME QUESTIONS AND ANSWERS

Question: Does this fundamental hierarchy and reciprocity exist only when teaching reading? *Answer:* No. Putting the subject matter in a specific order is an analytic methodology. Real life is not necessarily in a developmental order or hierarchy. All things are connected one way or another.

Question: Where are these fundamental reading skills practiced with respect to reading in general? *Answer:* Anywhere! Anytime! Anyplace! This could be in school, in your home, in a car, on a bus, airplane, at any grade level, on a train, at the zoo, by the lake, with a friend, or alone.

Question: What's your thought on the fundamentals of teaching reading and the ideas presented to you about them regarding hierarchy, and reciprocity? Take a moment or two to reflect and then share by writing your answer and conversing with a friend or colleague. Or hold onto the answer for a later sharing time.

IMPORTANT CHAPTER RELATIONSHIPS

The first six chapters are connected to part II of this book with respect to having explained the fundamentals of reading being evident throughout the book's sections. Specifically, the Reading Fundamentals section is present in part II's guidelines for oral reading presentation and silent reading directives. Each of these requires attention to the style of delivery or students being aware of the reading fundamentals when engaged in quiet time reading experiences. In that same section is chapter 8 which explains the layout and content of Different Reading Strategies in chapters 9–14. The Teaching Reading Fundamentals are then presented in every section of part III with the six different teaching reading strategies.

You may question how, and the answer would be that each chapter explains the strategy, how it is used in the classroom, and why it works with particular students' processing and/or learning styles, thereby establishing for whom the reading strategy is best suited. Then, there are lesson plans which emphasize all of the fundamentals and foundational components of teaching and learning, as presented in the Preface of this book, and are specifically addressed in the first six chapters.

Oh my, there is then parts IV and V that address teaching reading fundamentals through the presentation of positive character trait anecdotes and stories for reading and sharing. The book ends with appendices that include the author's closing thoughts for reflection about what's important in teaching and learning, and then the book's fundamentals and general foundations for teaching reading are evident in the closing Appendix B which has the author's career-reflective poetry. These were compiled over several decades of being a classroom teacher and university professor. It has been a rewarding experience . . . intertwined with lifetime realities, dreams, and wishes.

This entire book is an *interconnection* of all the chapters' content for preparing your students for success in reading! Where else? That would be in their daily encounters, for life, and the knowledge of their own self-worth being significant, certainly of such value as to share this information with others. In so doing, this book with different reading strategies builds classroom community that may well carry over to community outside of the school. As you read this book you will see the interplay of each chapter's content to realize that who we are is a conglomeration of each chapter as their content is in-play every day and in every way.

More Chapter Relationships: Each of the first six chapters of this book appears in the Reading Strategy's Lesson Plan section. This section contains an SEL activity as part of a lesson or an extension of it. Then, part IV's anecdotes on good character traits, as well as short stories in chapter 16 with chapter 6's five stages of a plot, are observable and utilized. It is here in these portions of the book that you will see the use of thinking with question asking, feelings with reactions to questions, or portions that call for opinions, thoughts, ideas, and even judgments.

Also, attention is given in each chapter to one's or whole groups' recalling something from their past experiences. That application is in reference to the three different forms of memory. Primarily, this consideration is given to the Activities or Differentiation of Instruction sections, and in some cases, ideas for Extending the Lesson.

Next, all the forms of comprehension are evident in the Activities segment of lesson plans. And finally, the parts of a story's plot are used when calling attention to a particular story or in part IV where Anecdotes and Short Stories reside. These short stories not only call for the students to realize a story's plot, through Exposition, Rising Action, Climax, Falling Action, and Resolution, but to the personalities of the characters in varied settings or the author's opinions, messages, or intent.

Author's Note: Social-emotional learning is in every aspect of teaching reading or any subject matter. It doesn't come last or necessarily in the middle or first part of teaching and learning. Social-emotional learning components are connected through the thinking and feelings of each learner in relation to life experiences. Over time, it is our experiential past that forms our present personality.

Acknowledgments

For this author it hardly seems possible to recognize all those who have been part of the creation of this book. And even more difficult is to acknowledge all those who helped shape my career in the teaching of thinking, reading, and social-emotional learning. There are teachers, administrators, and classmates who I taught and simultaneously taught me. That number would be in the thousand double-digit categories! Yes, there have been a multitude of people who influenced my career. And perhaps I should recognize public school #46 in upstate New York, for it was there that I didn't learn to read until age nine and decades later found that different strategies were needed for different students. It was those beginning years of "special education" that gave me the impetus to become a reading teacher. Overall, I needed to be one who knew her students' strengths to teach them the way they learn.

Next, two teachers in my high school years stand out as a huge influence on my doing well in school before and during tenth grade. The first is Ira Schulman who was, at the time, new to our school. He taught Algebra and caused me to overcome my fear of Math with his explaining it was like doing a puzzle. He encouraged participation and had an amiable nature with all of the class. Ms. Carragher once said to me, after I hadn't done particularly well on a social studies test, "Your strength is in listening and sharing, but certainly not test taking. Remember this. I believe in you." Those last four words caused me to wonder if I could believe in myself. Her comment impacted me to test the waters, so to speak, and develop self-reliance.

The college undergraduate years found a few professors who stood out and, I think, require acknowledgement in a generic way. This is with respect to their switching instruction from lecture to conversation. Most frequently this happened when there was something I didn't comprehend. Most simply stated, those that used a style of delivery that matched my learning and processing preferences worked best. Dr. Nissen, my sociology professor, is remembered as an individual who provided a good deal of classroom debate and discussion.

Going for my doctorate degree some twenty years later found my discovering not just a change in teaching styles but applying my teaching experience to instructional strategies of instructional leadership. It is here that I most profoundly recognize Dr. Rita Dunn, the originator, and head of that program at St. John's University. Not only was she guiding, but practiced the idea of praising one would yield their success in the program and encourage participation in a course, as well as teaching students. She modeled the three D's of teaching as mentioned in the very beginning of this book. Most importantly, Dr. Dunn practiced teaching students the way they learned and passed along that information in her courses and the doctorate program in general. She was and is held in high regard—forever.

Here at Molloy University, there are my colleagues who contributed to this book in anecdotes, or through their support of my writing endeavors. These include Bob Kinpoitner former chair of the English department who has been my grammarian for the nine books I have written. However, more importantly he is acknowledged for being a good friend with a phenomenal sense of humor, especially the pun type. There is then Michael Russo from Philosophy who encouraged my writing children's books. Also, as head of the Philosophy Department he encouraged debate and deep-thinking exercises to stimulate one's brain. And, former Molloy President, Drew Boger, joined with me in writing my first book. His interest in education was shared in numerous conversations about John Dewey's theory on adult education. He continually involved and engaged the students in practical application of one's individual knowledge which in 2020 led to his contributing a chapter in the book about preventing violence in schools.

When I first came to Molloy, I was assigned a mentor. Barbara Hayes was that individual and we shared ideas on teaching effectively from our personal perspectives as Barbara was a school administrator before becoming a college professor. We collaborated and continue to do that even after she retired several years ago. Then, as people come and go from the university scene there are those who influenced me with their camaraderie. Conversations here and there, showing an interest in what was happening with my writing or family, as we exchanged perspectives on a variety of topics. These people would require a listing of fifty persons. And so, I shall generically thank those in the School of Education and Human Services, and all administrative assistants in the offices they occupy at the university. Over my twenty-four years at Molloy, they have been friendly greeters, givers of information and all with a pleasant nature. Jasmine Holman and Charles Harmon at Rowman & Littlefield are appreciated for their correspondence and publishing expertise, as is

David Bailey for being remarkably caring in his conversational and written responses to my questions. Mahesh Meiyazhagan is acknowledged for the very fine reading and revisional work on this manuscript.

Friendships form as here and there are those persons who influenced my life and writing this book. They include graphic artist and illustrator of children's books Alan Gurwitz. He steadfastly assisted in sharing his views on teaching and the importance of caring about students. Then, there is Alan Offen who provided me the opportunity to edit his manuscript about his being a matrimonial lawyer. That experience proved to be very valuable as it took this author from a comfort zone to experience a new level of reading, novel style. Also included in this grouping of friends who stood by to be helpful are Angela Sullivan and high school days friends Joan Byrne and Oke Carhart. These three individuals have shared their beliefs and values, funny stories, as well as viewpoints on life's circumstances. This has been done openly and honestly on a variety of topics, and with reciprocity . . . who could ask for more, certainly not me.

Stepping back in time to 2008 would have me mention Tom Koerner, PhD, former editor and vice president of Educational Books from Rowman & Littlefield Publishers.

Happenstance presented this person to me, as I wrote in this section of my 2016 book on teaching critical and creative thinking: "Tom's publishing insight, based on his knowledge and foresight, guided me to writing my first book, and the ones after that as well. He is a most pleasant individual with a demeanor that connotes an interest in education and helping provide books to stimulate an individual's growth and development. I would think this extends to his overall being a person of good character who I had the fortune to meet over a decade ago. Thank you, Tom, for your guidance.

Of course, there is acknowledgment of my parents, Mollie and Red After. I clearly recall my dad asking me during winter break if I was going to work full time after high school or go to college. I was unsure, but he and mom led me to seek a college education. Interestingly, I wound up teaching college full time. There is friend Daisy Schneider, brother Ed After, and his wife Joan to be mentioned as friends and then, with great appreciation, is my husband, George. He is my technology person, supporter, encourager, and life partner. Our children and their spouses, as well as their children have also been a guiding beacon when it comes to supporting my writing endeavors. The last of this group refer to me as the best storyteller—isn't that what all books are, the story of our lives?

These individual's include Matt and Maddy, Alyssha and Paul Miro, Josh, Jolie, Mara and Dave Moore, and Seth and Carolina. Grandchildren-wise, there are Jared, Rayna, Eliana, Sam, Jonas, Jacob, Bailey, Marina, Landyn, Eva, Cameron, Levi, Jewel, and Caleb. My nephew Jonathan Borkum and niece Debbie Goss are also acknowledged for staying in contact and being encouraging. Lastly, I recognize the nearly 15,000 students I have taught at the elementary, middle school, and university levels. While I have taught them, I have equally learned from them the meaning and value of being in the field of education. Thank you.

Introduction

In this book the author is having, on many occasions, a conversation with the reader. In the middle of a chapter, there may appear reflection questions or ones that address analyzing what's being read/said. A sentence might appear like "What's your thought on that concept of academics incorporating students' social and emotional responses?" Then, instructions follow with "Share your thought(s) with another, and if someone isn't around, jot down your thoughts, ideas, opinions, or feelings for a later collaboration." This type of writing allows the reader to have a voice and know that this book is reader-friendly.

A key feature in chapter 6 of this book is a *Getting Acquainted* activity to use in your classroom at any time of the year and even may be repeated as weeks and months transpire. The beginning chapter of this book addresses knowing what one is thinking. This skill is provided for finite comprehension of a story through thought processes in a hierarchal/leveled and reciprocal/simultaneous fashion. A chart is provided for varied thinking skills' increasing complexity but realized as being simultaneous in practice. The chapter is titled "What Are You Thinking?" By knowing different types of thinking and recognizing your thoughts, it is possible to construct meaning from a read or listened-to story.

There are ample opportunities in this book to use one's metacognitive as well as creative and critical thinking skills that lead to self-actualization, or going forward and doing something—taking action. But most importantly the pages of this book provide the reader with the opportunity to be empowered and develop self-efficacy or reliance on oneself. This is accomplished through socialization techniques, such as discussion, debate, comparing of ideas, and overall sharing. In the long run, this communication aptitude is realized by valuing one's own skills and demonstrating that ability to communicate effectively. There is the practice of giving author's overt and subliminal examples to classmates, friends, teachers, and/or teachers to colleagues with one's innate comprehension of one's motivation to achieve. In fact, each of us can give what we first have to ourselves, meaning abilities, character traits, as much as material objects and subject matter.

You, the reader of this book, will become self-reliant in varied thinking skills. You'll develop an awareness that there are also types and uses of memory, academic and social cognition, and character traits with anecdotes. Stories for use with reading strategies are an additional area with which you'll become familiar, as well as for whom each strategy is best suited to students' needs. Not to be left out are the following points to enhance your teaching reading skills:

1. Processing style preference knowledge for determining a particular effective reading strategy for a student. Or at least physical accommodation and general expectations based on the students' brain hemisphere dominance. This includes (Dunn and Dunn, 1978–2008) *a student's preference or lack thereof* concerning learning new material. Such things as room design, illumination, sound, structure, working with adults, completing projects, working on one or several assignments simultaneously, and taking breaks or remaining on target are to be considered. A preference for science and math as opposed to the humanities is also connected to brain dominance or dual hemispheric preferences in accordance with the R. Dunn (1996; 2015) processing style philosophy.
2. Explaining reading strategy's components.
3. "Realizing one's emotional involvement in subject matter influences what will be recalled . . . what will be retained/learned" (Gurwitz, 2022).
4. Knowing why a particular reading strategy will work with one or several students but not all student learners.
5. Realizing that "*learning* is not a specific activity; or something a person does when not doing something else. No, it is not something individuals stop to do it, but rather the process of taking in information everywhere and at different levels, individually, collectively, and socially" (Wenger, 1998).
6. Acknowledging that, "Learning is basically a byproduct of thinking in a hierarchy with mutuality simultaneously realized. Then too there is retaining material to be used at another time, as use of one's memory is experienced. This may be in a classroom or any place you may be that involves information processing respective of what has been presented in verbal, as well as nonverbal formats. And in that time and space you

may alter the information to suit the situation . . . interacting with the individual's memories" (Schiering, 2003).
7. Adapting teaching and learning with the realization we do not all learn the same thing, the same way, at the same time.
8. Discovering components of varied Reading Strategies and Lesson Plans. This is with purposes, such as the reason for a topic and ultimate self-efficacy. Additionally, learning Practical Application with Activities and Questions, how character and social-emotional learning (SEL) are connected to academics, and ways to integrate these into a specific lesson plan are given attention.
9. Using a SEL activity for each lesson plan that focuses on the concept of creating a cohesive group of learners interested in sharing what they know.
10. Integrating the topics into a totally inclusive environment where occupants feel successful, accepted, and in harmony with those in that shared space.

This last skill is accomplished through providing topic-based information, as well as presenting different reading strategies. Then, there are the comprehension and integration of character development skills with SEL presented in lesson plans and activities that address lesson objectives. Also provided are ways to *model behaviors* that enhance classroom participation through positive-based communication skills. These skills are meant to be all-encompassing so that each student learner has a sense of togetherness with classmates. As one teaches, one learns and as one learns, one teaches. Everyone is a teacher of "something," and that "something" is one's "character" (Schiering, Spring 2009).

Author's Note: This book is partially designed to have you examine ways to make that demonstration of character a positive one. You may question, "Where?" The answer is, in an academic setting as it is there that students practice caring about subject matter and others to establish harmony.

REGARDING SEL

SEL is addressed in this book with the goal of developing self-awareness and self-control, while capitalizing on interpersonal communication skills. These are vital for, not just the school, but home, work, community, and life success. A major factor for SEL is learning to talk "with" others and having a sense of self-appreciation where you are liking you.

When it comes to knowing about reading strategies' names and components, one must also know for whom this strategy works and why that is the case. In this book, within the presentation of each specific reading strategy is included reading strategy objectives, activities, labeled questions for the three types of comprehension, thinking skills, and specified student learners' verbal discourse designed to develop SEL. Each chapter's end has a section on "Character Counts with SEL."

REGARDING CHARACTER DEVELOPMENT COUNTS

This book emphasizes the importance of teaching character development for enhanced communication in the classroom; talking "with" one another, as opposed to one's speaking "at" someone or "to" someone with a lecture. Character development is exemplified through sharing book contributor's experiences using anecdotes involving such concepts as being kind, trustworthy, fair, caring, open-minded, accepting, showing good citizenship, and the like.

Additionally, there is a chapter on short stories that may stimulate SEL through sharing the situation presented in the story and how it was addressed. Students are encouraged to express their ideas and have discussions about not just a story's content, but the possible author's intent and messages the story conveys both overtly and subliminally.

The main concept for this positive type of instruction is to establish a sense of "unity" in the classroom. Unity as also in the word Community requires "U" = You (Schiering, M. S. Schiering, M. R., 2022).

BOOK'S AUDIENCE

This book is for you, regardless of your job/professional title. It's for you because the subject involves reading and the ways to go about learning to read. And it focuses on the impact your past and present experiences in this field had on you that shaped the "you" of now. That information is empowering as you come to understand your own personality. And, if you are in the education field, this book is for you as it addresses teaching reading fundamentals and various teaching-reading strategies that have SEL as a component.

These include SEL and its connection to everyday experiences in the classroom setting. Your personality and character, have been shaped by your life situations. The you of now rely on those times and memories of them. Subsequently, you bring your character to every situation, and it is that character that serves as a teacher of who you are. Subsequently, this

Introduction xxiii

book is for anyone of any age, grade, socio-economic level, race, religion, and so on.

In the educational field, this book is for those who want to engage student learners in viable, enjoyable instruction. This teaching technique comes with addressing what's suited to students' needs, because of their personal involvement in learning. It's for wonderment in learning by using different means of instruction and realizing that any academic situation encompasses socialization along with feelings, senses, and emotions. In that vein, this book is for:

1. Instituting and maintaining student learners' interests, security, and application of differentiation of instructional methodologies.
2. Providing learning experiences that may include technology and most importantly preparing your students for success. Do you know what that is? It's intrinsically knowing what instructional strategies work for whom, as well as when to use them.
3. Building self-efficacy is a goal as much as you, the educator, appreciating yourself, and recognizing how to build an inclusive classroom.

AUTHOR'S PHILOSOPHY

- One reading strategy does not necessarily work for all students.
- What we think and feel becomes what we say and do.
- Memory impacts one's character, and SEL is present in and outside the classroom.
- We learn and teach simultaneously, and we're all teachers of our dispositions and demeanors.
- Engagement in the learning process allows for the most effective retention of material.
- The educational setting must be a comfort zone for optimum learning to happen to create community and unity through you as teacher and student.
- Conversations need to be "with" others as opposed to "at" or "to" them so that the experience is all inclusive.
- One classroom rule should be continually practiced and it's, "No put downs, Only lift ups!" This rule applies to students' conversations and those with oneself as well. Putting yourself or anyone down with negative statements serves no purpose. There is nothing to be gained by doing that" (Schiering, 1976/ 2015).
- Using instruction that meets the needs of classroom student learners, self-acceptance is likely to follow. Self-acceptance comes with the ingrained concept of, "I am enough as I am."

Part I

TEACHING READING FUNDAMENTALS

Each of the following six chapters defines, in practice, the terms teaching and learning. Each is a part of the other—an interconnection. Grouped together in such a manner as to be reciprocal and happening simultaneously, these form the fundamentals for teaching reading.

Chapter 1

What Are You Thinking?

THINKING IS COGNITION

Well, you probably knew that the word "thinking" is a synonym for cognition. And in a sentence, you might ask about one's cognitive ability and mean how does one do thinking or at thinking. What may not come readily to mind is that there are numerous types of thinking and that these are different from feelings. Nonetheless, what is your answer when someone asks you, "What are you thinking?" The customary response is to say what is on your mind at that given moment. Let's say the question is asked at dinner time and your response is, "I'm thinking about how much I'm going to enjoy the pizza you ordered." Simple question and just as easy a response.

Thinking for the purpose of answering a question is a direct response using thoughts you're having on the topic presented. What if there isn't a specific question or topic? What might you be thinking? Perhaps you're reflecting on a past experience, or you're wondering about a future one, or your mind is blank. What are you thinking now? Please, jot it down for later reference. And as you read this chapter or other ones in this book, you're invited to record in a journal any thoughts you're having.

In the finite sense, *thinking refers to the ability of the brain to process, store, retrieve, and manipulate information.*

One more thing: "We are our thinking and feelings from our earliest memories of our home, school, friendships, etc with mental and verbal discourse, to every circumstance in the present. So, following that line of thinking, it's noted that: 'What we think and feel, at some point, becomes what we say and do' based on our personal histories" (Schiering, © 1999; 2017; 2023).

THE HIERARCHY OF THINKING

The most popular belief is that thinking is done developmentally. As one matures there is thinking that occurs at a specified level from a lower to higher order. The concept of give and take within the development process is not necessarily realized. No, the idea is that as the child develops the instruction comes from the top down in a specified dissemination-of-information manner. A structure is in place with babies at the lowest level of cognition. Lev Vygotsky (1978) challenged this idea with one that addressed sociocultural learning. The concept he related, in simplistic terms, stated that cognition develops with the social exchange of thoughts (Vygotsky 1986, 2015). Sociocultural theory views human development as a socially mediated process in which children acquire their cultural values, beliefs, and problem-solving strategies through collaborative dialogues with more knowledgeable members of society. Other theorists explain that children's development must necessarily precede their learning. Is either one, correct? Is there only one way?

THE RECIPROCITY OF THINKING

Please follow along with me here. If one thinks in a progressive/sequential way from lowest thinking to highest thinking, is there a crossover at any point? In her 1999 doctoral dissertation, following a good deal of research, Schiering developed a chart to relate that while thinking moves from beginning awareness to critical and creative thinking and then metacognitive processes, there is, in fact, continual thinking done *within and between* these levels.

On upcoming pages, examples are given. These show a chart where thinking is categorized into three phases, thus forming a hierarchy. However, due to some thinking skills coming from each phase in any given situation, the thinking is reciprocal. This reciprocity is evident with an exchange, not of every thinking skill, but some of them occurring simultaneously on a regular basis. How this happens is presented in a story format a few paragraphs from here. However, first, let's address knowing what you're thinking. Identification of thinking skills is a form of *teaching thinking*, as it puts you in a place to identify the skills in relation to real life, reading texts or reading in any school discipline.

KNOWING WHAT YOU'RE THINKING

The following definitions of thinking skills, with examples of each one, are provided to distinguish one from the other, contextually. So what? You may say, and the answer is that it is these that define us within our present. What one thinks and feels forms a personality and one's character and impacts one's academic abilities.

Here's an aside concept: We are all teachers, regardless of having that title placed upon us because of receiving instruction in that field. Whether a manicurist, dentist, grocery store clerk, doctor, nurse, hairdresser, and the list could continue. Truth be known, "We are all teachers of something and that something is our character" (Schiering, 1999). Our thinking and feelings form that character. Our thinking and feelings shape others' opinions of us, based on what we say and how we act.

Since we all are teachers of our character, then we obviously share that when we teach. We model thoughts, ideas, opinions, and judgments on a regular basis. As a beginning activity in this chapter on thinking, let's see if you can distinguish the differences between the following definitions and give examples yourself. Then, share them with students and have them work collaboratively or individually with a follow-up sharing of their examples. The class, joining with the teacher, then is involved in social-emotional learning.

FOUR TYPES OF THINKING: DEFINITIONS

- THOUGHTS: Immediate conscious responses to reflection, which involve memory. Example: I'm thinking we might go to the beach today.
- IDEAS: A prediction of future responses or speculation based on one's perception, as a result of reflection. Example: My idea is that after school I'll work out by going bicycle riding.
- OPINIONS: A combination of thoughts and ideas that result in a formulated concept. Example: It's my opinion that winter is coming, as I see the leaves falling off the trees.
- JUDGMENTS: Concretized thoughts, ideas, opinions, which are impacted by memory. Example: Kind people are nice to be around (Schiering & Bogner, 2007).

IDENTIFYING THINKING SKILLS: THE TEACHING OF THINKING

Reciprocal Thinking Activity: Practicing Knowing What You're Thinking
Materials: A storyteller, a storybook (picture or chapter) textbook in any discipline or writing assignment in any discipline.
Prompt . . . When Were You . . . .

Assignment: In written format use each of the thinking skills to demonstrate when you are aware that thinking skill was being addressed in a specified story. You may use one from chapter 15. This activity demonstrates one's ability to know what thinking was happening and recognizing that for edification. Of course, you'll need the chart and the thinking skills that are on it as your guide. If you find another thinking skill not on the chart, share it and determine what phase it represents.

"PHASE ONE: *Recognizing*: Taking notice of words or actions. *Realizing*: Where you are, what will be. *Classifying*: Having an order to things. *Comparing*: Naming similarities. *Contrasting*: Naming differences.

"PHASE TWO: *Prioritizing*: The act of showing preferential sequencing. *Communicating*: Talking with another. *Inferring/Active Listening*: Using indirect evidence and contributing to a conversation. *Predicting*: Guessing what will happen next based on written or read material's content. *Generalizing*: Realizing that most people feel, think, or do what's related in the material presented, Sequencing: organizing the chronology of events. *Initial-deciding and Problem-solving*: Locating one or two choices to be made as a result of the reading or writing and then taking action.

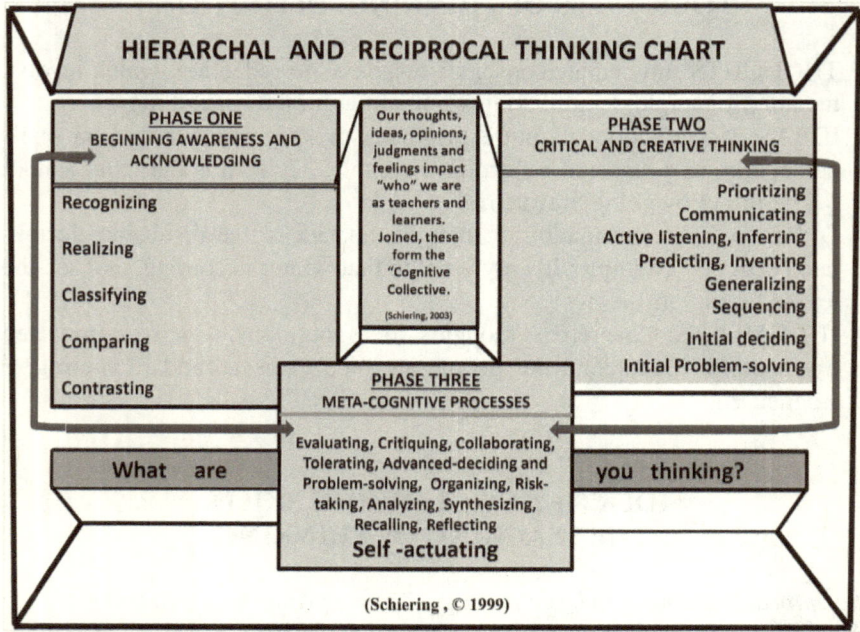

Figure 1.1 Hierarchical and Reciprocal Thinking Phases. *Source:* Schiering, 1999.

"*PHASE THREE: Evaluating*: Formatting an idea and assessing the situation. *Critiquing*: Doing an analytic assessment of a specific section or overall scope of the material. *Collaborating*: Working "with" others through conversation, writing, or projects. *Advanced deciding/Problem-solving and Organizing*: Identifying and concluding beliefs, values, and actions and doing this while putting things in a pattern or sequence. *Risk-taking*: Being adventuresome in trying something new and challenging, an action often equated with trying something in thought or deed. *Inventing*: Creating something new from what's been presented in reading, writing, or tactile/ kinesthetic formats.

"*Analyzing:* The act of scrutinizing, examining, and possible dissecting a problem or general situation by using deep thinking strategies. *Synthesizing*: Joining of one's thoughts and ideas, opinions, and judgments, as well as feelings. *Recalling*: Remembering a situation from the past that was made evident by one's emotional experience with that situation. With respect to a book being read, paper written, or the like, this thinking skill may first require comparing and contrasting what's presented to one's own experiences. *Reflecting*: Looking back on the relevance of what's presented.

"*Self-actualizing:* Going forward and taking action. This could be something as simple as walking across a room. Or self-actuating may involve many of the aforementioned thinking skills to provide information for going forward and taking action, doing something" (Schiering, 1999).

EXAMPLE OF PRE-LANGUAGE THINKING USING THE CHART

TWO SCENARIOS TO DEMONSTRATE PRE-LANGUAGE THINKING

1. A toddler is on the floor where two objects have been placed. This is a child, still at the crawling but not walking stage of development. There are two visible objects on the floor. The child, Tom, crawls over to the first one, which is a very small toy car. What does the child do? Naturally, he puts the toy car in his mouth. Discovering this action doesn't feel good, the child takes out the little metal car and puts it back on the floor.

Next, the 10-month-old sees a marshmallow on the floor and crawls over to it. Where does he put the marshmallow? Naturally, he puts this tasty treat in his mouth and eats it. Now, fast-forward a few days or more and that same child is in the same situation. However, this time the toddler bypasses the toy car. Where does the child go? Naturally, the child goes to the marshmallow and puts it in his mouth to eat.

The cognitive beginning awareness, critical and creative thinking, as well as meta-cognitive skills you witnessed were as follows: recognizing there were objects on the floor, realizing these may be tasty but needing to get to them required crawling over to them. Comparing and contrasting took places with putting the toy car into his mouth and realizing it didn't feel good. Subsequently, removes the toy car from the mouth. Crawling to the other object on the floor, the toddler repeats the action as he classifies this as being different from the toy car. Then, tasting this delight, the child eats the marshmallow. What happened, thinking wise was prioritizing, early decision making, taking a risk, evaluating, recalling, and reflecting on this new object, and then, self-actualizing with the eating of the marshmallow. One might say that communicating was evidenced by the toddler eating the marshmallow.

Same scene a few days or a week later and the child goes past the toy car. As memory is involved, which is recalling that tasting the car wasn't a good feeling the toddler bypasses this object and goes on to the marshmallow, which is then eaten. The same cognitive skills from each phase were observable as the toddler evaluated the objects. Both times were the cognitive skills of analyzing the scene, risk-taking by putting objects in the mouth, recalling, reflecting, and self-actuating when eating the marshmallow.

By observing the actions of the toddler, you can realize that the child is thinking *simultaneously within and between* the hierarchal and reciprocal thinking Phases. Additionally, the use of his memory was continually clear when the scene was repeated.

YOUR TURN: PRE-LANGUAGE THINKING

2. A five-month-old baby is being fed dinner in a highchair: Some foods are welcomed with verbalizations of "Oh, Ah, Mm" and a smiley face, while others are rejected by putting up a hand to push away the offered food, or perhaps there are crying and a sad face.

Question: What phases are represented in this baby's facial expressions and limited verbiage, and what skills are shown within those phases?
Hint: Here are the phases with only one skill being noted. Let's see if you can find other skills and label them by Phase 1, 2, or 3.

1. *Beginning Awareness*: Even with this limited scenario in pre-language thinking, the baby is *recognizing* that food is being presented for eating.
2. *Critical and Creative Thinking*: The baby showed a smiley face.

3. *Metacognitive Processes*: The baby *evaluated* the food by showing signs of pushing it away and showing a sad face.

Now, please take out your notebook or paper and record what other thinking skills of the baby you observed, or thought were being evidenced.

Q: What are you thinking now?

Please take a moment; look at what you put in your notes for what you were thinking at the start of this chapter. Next, write down what you're thinking now, and/or compare the start of this "Knowing what you're thinking" topic to your beginning awareness, critical and creative thinking . . . such as how you might apply this to everyday experiences, as well as any metacognitive processes you noted.

Let's share if there is time to do this.

APPLYING THE THINKING SKILLS IN THE CLASSROOM

First: Know the definition of each thinking skill. Exemplify each skill so it can be addressed in verbal or written format when reviewing the story.

Second: Use identification of thinking in storytelling, decision-making, research, narratives, writing, varied literacy components, and reading in all disciplines. Be sure to know the meaning of each hierarchal and reciprocal thinking skill and identify when the thinking skills were applied in the story.

Third: Tell or write a story and practice identification of the thinking skills that were addressed. Use the hierarchal and reciprocal thinking skills chart in any discipline.

Finally: Knowing what you're thinking becomes a natural process through practice. The one who knows what is being thought *develops self-reliance and self-efficacy + empowerment. Go for it!*

BEFORE THE "FEELINGS" IN CHAPTER 2

As you are about to embark on the next chapter of this book, which addresses "feelings," there is one important notation this author chooses to bring forward as an introduction to the idea that thinking and feelings are not the same, as the latter deals with emotions, whereas the former may not. Here's the important notation: Thinking and feelings are not the same thing. While they may impact one's comprehension, their interpretation may be different.

IMPORTANT NOTATIONS

1. Thinking does not necessarily equate with feelings.
2. Feelings often supersede thinking as perceptions are involved in a sensory and emotional format.
3. Feelings may or may not be classified or able to be described, as they are simply experienced within oneself.
4. Some feelings are evidenced by all individuals and at or nearly at the same time. An example would be the sensation of loving.

ONE MORE IMPORTANT NOTATION

In this chapter you have examined, in a finite manner, information about thinking. One area of importance for teaching thinking is to identify what you are thinking. This author recognizes that once verbalization of thinking occurs, rarely does one dissect or identify all the thoughts one is having. Nor does one examine if something was a thought, idea, opinion, or judgment.

This thinking comes naturally, and one does not say something like, I was prioritizing when this happened, and using sequencing when . . . That's okay, it's natural not to do that. But this chapter has related how to do that "knowing what you're thinking" so the individual will understand how knowing what one's thinking helps with reading.

You don't need to say what you're thinking aloud, but making mental notes of it allows for self-efficacy and empowerment. That knowledge is gained because you come to know yourself and what you're reading by your identification of the thinking terms, process, and implementation within a read item or everyday situation.

Suggestion: Empower your students as you empower yourself by knowing what thinking skills you are implementing.

CHAPTER QUESTIONS

1. What is a synonym for thinking?
2. What is the definition of thinking? How do you apply that in your classroom?
3. What are examples of each of the four types of thinking?
4. What does it mean to have thinking in a hierarchy? How would you explain that concept?

5. What does reciprocity of thinking mean?
6. What are the three phases of thinking, as presented on the "chart?" What is your reaction to teaching thinking?
7. Do you believe that everyone has the right to think and if so, why? If not, why not?
8. Why is thinking an important part of reading and how might you teach thinking in a classroom?
9. What are your thoughts on pre-language thinking?
10. What are you thinking now? Explain your answer.

Chapter 2

What Are You Feeling?
Distinguishing Thinking from Feeling

FEELING INVOLVES EMOTION

Unlike chapter 1, this chapter focuses on "Feelings." There are only two types of feelings: sensory ones and emotional ones. A definition goes like this:

FEELINGS: A sensory and/or emotional response to stimuli that may be a descriptive or classificatory account of a situation that involves sentiment or physicality. (Schiering & Bogner, 2007)

Example: I felt excited (emotion) when my team won the baseball game. Subsequently, my hands stung (sensory) when I clapped vigorously at their winning.

MYRIAD OF FEELINGS

There is no getting around it. There are so many feelings that to list them in a chart or categorize them is nearly impossible. But one thing is for sure: "feelings are reciprocal, and not necessarily experienced in a hierarchy manner" (Schiering, 1986). You may question that, but let's take a look at feeling words and realize that these could occur at any time and are not reliant on any sort of developmental theory.

Therefore, in the next titled area, feeling words have been listed under the heading of "The Experience of Being." Since there are so many words listed, this author decided to put them in groups of three. This grouping is for the sake of organization and so you, the book's reader, do not simply have sixty-five words bunched together in a paragraph. These feeling words may be experienced at any time and are not in a particular order. One further thought is that feelings are neither right nor wrong, they just are.

FEELING WORDS

The "Experience of Being . . . Feeling:"

"GROUP ONE: Aware, attentive, acknowledging, understanding, responsive, organized, relaxed, loving, appreciative, different, similar, caring, satisfied, happy, sad, content, concerned, interested, explorative, lonely, excited, curious, imaginative.

"GROUP TWO: Communicative, enthralled, imaginative, mystified, open, decisive, unrestrained, intrigued, questioning, supportive, resourceful, funny, creative, positive, critical, predictive, engaging, controlled, exhilarated, uncertain, inspired, connected.

"GROUP THREE: Evaluative, contented, empathetic, condolatory, collaborative, tolerant, sympathetic, adventuresome, inventive, analytical, holistic, critiquing, constructive, disquieted, participatory, discerning, reflective, and self-actuating." (Schiering, 2008)

DISTINGUISHING THINKING FROM FEELINGS

There is a relatively simple way to distinguish stating what you're thinking, as opposed to what you're feeling. The idea of doing that originated when one of this author's English classes was doing creative writing about the topic of "A time when." The teacher returned the papers a few days after the students submitting them, and related that many of them expressed thoughts as feelings. She said, *"If you can substitute the words, 'I am' for 'I feel' and the sentence makes sense, then you have expressed a feeling,"* Otherwise, you've likely stated a thought. When one knows about different types of thinking, one realizes that choosing words that express thoughts, ideas, opinions, or judgments are different from those that express feelings.

You are now aware of knowing about four different types of thinking. And you're also aware of there being two different forms of feelings. Hopefully, you likely realize that by using this "substitution" of *I am* for *I feel,* and the sentence making sense, provides a clear example of differentiating between thoughts and sensory or emotional feelings. Anyway, here are some examples of this guideline applied to a few sentences:

EXAMPLES OF FEELINGS VERSUS THOUGHTS

1. I feel that you should answer that question. I am that you should answer that question. Ah, the writer has expressed a *thought*, as substituting the

word "am" for "feel" causes the sentence not to make sense. *Thought expressed.*
2. I feel uneasy when answering questions. I am uneasy when answering questions. Yup, the sentence is correct with the substitution of the word "am" for "feel." *Feeling expressed!*
3. I feel opposed to your joining the team. I am opposed to you joining the team. *Feeling expressed.*
4. I feel excited about driving the car for the first time. I am excited about you driving the car for the first time. *Feeling expressed.*
5. I feel chilled when the winter winds blow and feel I best wear a coat when going outside. I *am chilled* when the winter winds blow and am I best wear a coat when going outside. Ah, we've a compound sentence where the first statement of feeling chilled is a feeling. However, the second part of the sentence with what is best to wear is an example of thinking, and should read, . . . and think I best wear a coat when going outside.

Very simply, in the class where I learned about this object lesson, we redid our papers for sharing with the class and the creative writing stories were fascinating. This was as much a grammatical success as it was one where our imagination abounded in writing. There was a wide range of experiences expressed in our creative writing endeavors.

When these were read aloud in our class, we came to know our classmates on a different level than doing a math equation or science experiment or recalling an historical event. Although not titled as such, back then this writing assignment with sharing was a social-emotional learning experience, as we talked with one another about ourselves with respect to what we'd written.

NOW, IT'S YOUR TURN TO TRY: CLASSROOM ACTIVITY

You're asked to go back to the examples given for types of thinking and try to create sentences with a partner or by yourself to share later that express a thought, then an idea, next an opinion and judgment. When it comes to emotional or sensory feelings, you're asked to create two sentences that do just that. Then, apply the substitution idea of "I am" for "I feel" and see if you have expressed a feeling. If you're in a classroom you could ask for sentences to be illustrated and construct a wall design with the pictures. Or, if your classroom has technology available do this substitution practice on a Smart Board or computer that others can see at an assigned time. Or you could print the examples students configure and distribute these to the class.

Oh, if you're doing the illustration idea, then try to have the sentence placed at the bottom of the picture so classmates may "read the wall display," as well as looking at what has been created, picture wise.

One more example: I feel bad that you're watching the football game today. I am bad that you're watching the football game today. *Thought expressed.*

IMPORTANT NOTATION REITERATED

1. Evidence may be required for a concrete thought that's not impaired by what one feels.
2. Thinking does not necessarily equate with feelings. The latter often supersedes the former.
3. Evidence may be required for concrete thought that's not impaired by what one feels.
4. Feelings just are. They are not right or wrong, but exist and may impact the way one thinks and/or what one thinks, whether it be ideas, opinions, judgments, or simply thoughts.

CHAPTER QUESTIONS

1. What are two types of feelings?
2. What distinguishes one from the other?
3. How can you tell, in written format, if someone has expressed a feeling or a thought?
4. Looking at each group of feeling words, select one from each group and provide a time when you felt that way. How does this activity make you feel and why?
5. How are you feeling now? What are you thinking? (This author is feeling happy. She thinks this section of the book reads well and is hoping readers will try the feel/am activity in their classrooms.)

Chapter 3

Memory Definition with Examples and Three Types of Memory

MEMORY EXPLANATION

Memory usage is the idea that in order to comprehend something, then one needs to reflect. The reflection (second highest skill in Phase 3) may be regarding the past or something that is newly presented. Generally speaking, or in this case "reading" reflection requires the following:

1. Going back in time to examine some situation or story,
2. Bringing it forward to the present,
3. Examining it,
4. Collecting your thoughts about it through recall and reflection,
5. Viewing one's feelings is at least one reason a person has a memory, and
6. Involving emotional recall and reflection with feelings results in one's emotional response, when it occurs, being significant. Then, a memory of it is formed.

Overall, "Ones memory involves a looking-back-in-time, experiencing analysis and evaluation (Metacognitive Skills) of some event or events. This is regardless of if the event was from a moment ago, and/or going further back and recalling what was read or said, experienced or felt. Then, there is a looking-forward while realizing (Basic Awareness Skills) some life experiences have made us who we are in the present. Memory influences personality characteristics for actions to be taken in the present or future and relies on past experience as well."

In that context, "*We are our experiential past. And people can only address, perceive particulars, configure generalities, respond through emotional venues to interpret what they find or found to be significant. This is done through reviewing their life involvements by incorporating–through reflection and recall of their previous experiences. All in all, one's points of reference are based upon their reflection"* (Schiering, 2000–to present).

Now you may be questioning how memory influences or impacts reading in a reading, language arts lesson, or any subject matter. If the experience of learning the presented material is noteworthy to the reader, then it is learned. Additionally, memories are shaped when a particular subject is presented in a way the students can identify and form a memory. The idea is that those memories influence one's comprehension and the experience of learning needs to be impactful.

EXAMPLE OF A MEMORY THAT BECAME A PORTION OF A STORYBOOK

The First Bicycle Ride

It was a typical warm fall day in a suburban neighborhood in Rochester, NY. The seven-year-old girl's dad had just offered to teach his daughter how to ride the two-wheeler that had sat in their garage for the past month. The bike had been her birthday gift and she was excited beyond belief to learn how to ride. Today, Monday, would be the day! Maggie was beyond belief excited as her dad took the bike to the "no-traffic" street in front of their house.

"Today's the day," her dad said, "You're going to learn to ride this red bicycle. Then, you can ride up the street instead of walking to Karen and Tom's house. Now, I will balance it and you get on and hold the handlebars. These are used for steering the bike. Next, I'll help you have a sense of balance by holding onto the back of the seat as you place your feet on the peddles. Finally, you are to peddle the bike and steer it while I run alongside you."

Confidently, and still with excitement and happiness, seven-year-old Maggie did as she was instructed, and things went exceptionally well. She steered, she peddled, and then picked up speed so the bicycle was going faster as her dad ran alongside, until he didn't. And when Maggie realized her dad couldn't keep up and had let go of the back of the bicycle seat, the steering wheel wobbled, the peddling stopped, the bike veered, as if on its own, but really steered by Maggie, to the right. It hit the curb, and she went flying across the sidewalk. Maggie was crying and very upset because she was bruised and even bleeding a bit. Her dad came running over and asked, "What happened?"

"You let go," his daughter replied. Dad answered, "How long did you think I could hold on? You were going so fast!"

"Until I was twelve!" Maggie answered.

Dad smiled and calmed his daughter. He said that she must have been joking, and she answered in the negative. She wanted him to hold on, and as she got older, she discovered that she let go very reluctantly of anything or anyone. Still, she had learned to ride the bike and did so not just to her friend's house up the street, but to other schoolmates in the neighborhood (Schiering, 1999–present).

SIMPLE REVIEW INVOLVING MEMORY APPLICATION

Topic: Learning to ride a bicycle.
Setting: Rochester, NY, in front of child's house in a residential neighborhood.
Characters: Seven-year-old child and her dad.
Moods: Excited, scared, adventuresome, and upset.

Author's Note: If students were doing a Story Map Graphic Organizer, each of these italicized sections would be filled-in with information from the story. Example of Moods: Excited mood was evidenced when starting to ride the bike, "scared" happened when the child knew dad had let go of the bike, "adventuresome" took place when starting to peddle faster, "upset" happened when the bike's steering wheel wobbled, and "renewed interest" occurred when trying to ride the bike another time.

STORY EXTENSION TO SCIENCE

After the story had been read in class, the teacher made a connection to a lesson on motion and balance to name only two topics. And, after that, the teacher explained that there are three types of memory (see the section titled "Three Types of Memory") accompanied by asking the class about their memories of first learning to ride a bicycle or something just as significant in their earlier years. This exercise brought about a good deal of classroom sharing, communication at its best! SEL at its best!

Some stories were told, and some were written out for reading at other times. The reiteration of how one learns to balance and what things can be balanced, as well as the aforementioned topic, were reviewed many times in the fifth-grade class. As time went by, it was the sharing that brought more memories. These were recalled and reflected upon for other assignments involving how thinking and feelings impact memory formation and influence our lives on a daily basis.

THREE TYPES OF MEMORY

1. Attention: the ability to focus on a specific stimulus without being distracted.
2. Orientation: the ability to be aware of self and certain realities and facts that configure, modify, or rearrange information. These correspond with the ability of a person to respond to stimuli and line-up with everyday life experiences.
3. Decision-making and Problem-solving: the ability to understand a problem, generate a solution or more than one, and evaluate these (Schiering, 2003).

Looking at these three types of memory, one sees that the focus of the Bicycle Riding story was on a specific incident: the first bike ride for Maggie. Additionally, the orientation was recalling where this experience took place, the feelings of the main character, and the facts of the event given in sequence. The decision-making was done with the commitment to try riding the bike and then the statement about how long Maggie expected her dad to be assistive. This decision was determined through her evaluation of the situation.

Author's Note: The story was used, in a college classroom, as a catalyst to engage students in memory and could be applied to any age-grade level, as it's a *common experience* type of story. The relating of incidents emphasized memory, and the topics from science were then introduced for learning about what's involved in bicycle riding. These topics then could be extended to ELA with story writing and math with asking questions about estimating how many revolutions of the wheel took place over a stated period of time. Subsequently, the sharing of a story brought about social-emotional learning as students reacted to the story events with active listening.

EIGHT GENERAL QUESTIONS FOR USE OF MEMORY, UNDERSTANDING/COMPREHENSION, AND COGNITION/THINKING

Whole-Class, Partnership, or Small-Group Formats

1. When did you learn to read and write, and what was that like for you?
2. What was your feeling type reaction to early school years, and why do you think that was the case?
3. What's learning like now for you?

4. What was funny to you two, five, ten years ago, and what's funny to you now? Why do you think that reaction is true?
5. Who are three people, aside from your family members, that you like? Why do you think you like them? Is there a common trait and if so, what is it?
6. What motivates you to learn? What impact does teaching, or the teacher, have on your life?
7. Now that you know the three types of memories, what are two memories that you have that you think are interest areas for others?
8. How would you form these into a story to be told or written?

REVIEW AND WHAT'S NEXT

This chapter has dealt with understanding with the presentation and exemplification of types of memory and their significance in impacting an individual's comprehension. As examples we were given scenarios and then questions to stimulate use of one's memory were presented. The three forms of "memory" were given attention and more questions provided to engage one in thinking back in time to things recalled, because of their emotional significance. What comes in the next chapter is comprehension or understanding of what has been read. Chapters 1–3 lead to reading for comprehension.

CHAPTER QUESTIONS

1. What are the three types of understanding or comprehension?
2. Which one, as a student, is easiest to access and why is it learned?
3. What are the three forms of memory?
4. What were two things you recalled from your past that had emotional significance?
5. How and why does understanding subject matter, such as reading and memory, impact your learning?
6. How do you suppose one's emotional feelings impact one's learning?
7. How do you suppose one's experiential past influences one's present self?

Chapter 4

Reading Involves Understanding = Comprehension

COMPREHENSION = UNDERSTANDING

Looking at the title of this chapter may bring a series of questions to your mind. Is this author asking about what you understand and, if so, on what topic? Or is she asking if you comprehend understanding? Since the words are synonymous, it's difficult to make a distinction as to what is being asked.

Ask yourself how you know someone "understands" something said, read, taught, or presented. In everyday conversations, someone says, "Do you understand that?" The response most normally is. "Do I understand? Of course, you want to know if I realize how important what you said was, and I do." Simple question and simple answer with restating the topic and giving affirmation without a "why" is the answer.

More times than not, the reason for that quick answer is to avoid thinking and just let things be as they are. Who wants conflict? Who wants more questions or reasoning to be required for an answer? Few! However, when asking if someone understands, aside from the answer provided, how do you know that understanding has been achieved? Customarily, in the classroom, the answer to that question is to give a test and see how many things were understood by the number of right and/or wrong answers.

However, overall, comprehension or understanding something involves memory. Therefore, memory involves storing and then recalling and retrieving thoughts and feelings. This recalling is the step before reflection where time is spent analyzing what is remembered. Memory examples are provided at the close of this chapter.

Most thinking consciously or unconsciously involves recalling stored information. One's recalling is based on the emotional significance of the topic being presented. If it was going to the zoo, for example, the memory may be strong as it would be a place not often frequented. Understanding of a visit to a zoo would be rather profound. However, going to school and remembering each event of any given day probably wouldn't be so important to cause a memory to form. Also, if you're interested in a subject area, then the retention of information is usually good, and understanding is evidenced through your participation in the lesson being taught. Yes, a test may yield fact-based retention of information, but not necessarily the essence of the topic addressed.

"One's understanding/comprehension is a main goal of education and the encompassing basis of the formation of personalities through grasping concepts, ideas, thoughts, opinions, and emotional reactions to stimuli" (Schiering, 2017).

SCENARIO ABOUT UNDERSTANDING = COMPREHENSION

The teacher reads a book to the class. It was a children's picture book. The class being read to was at the fifth-grade level, and as each page is read, the colors of the pictures were responded to with such statements as "Oh, nice." The big issue was why a picture book is not being read to a younger class. The teacher initially explained that the message at the end of the book is appropriate for any age person, even an adult.

Mrs. D., the teacher, explains that the format is for what most considered a younger grade level, but the message is for everyone. The story, *Sammy Snail's A Little Time for Quiet,* has part of the text provided. The questions that follow the poem-formatted book address different types of understanding or comprehension to know if the reader or listener has understood the story.

"Sammy snail was very slow.
He glided over streets.
He talked about the daily sounds
With everyone he'd meet.
"It's true" he said, "I'm very sad.
I don't know what to say.
It seems the noise around me
is getting worse each day."
"Some noise must stop," he simply said.
"It's more than I can stand."
So, Sammy Snail went on is way
To ask for . . . a quiet land.
He went right up to Buddy Bullfrog
Who lived just over there.

Reading Involves Understanding = Comprehension 25

> *And, he asked him to be helpful and*
> *Please do his fair share.*
> *"I see." Said Buddy bullfrog.*
> *"then here's what we must do.*
> *Go over to the train yard*
> *and down around the zoo."*
> *We'll tell everyone and everything*
> *The best way they will hear*
> *That we need a 'time for quiet'.*
> *Let's make it very clear."*
> *Sammy and Buddy go to many places and ask for*
> *quiet. The book ends with this verse:*
> *So, Sammy Snail went near and far*
> *And softly said, "Please try it.*
> *Let's have a part of every day*
> *With a little time for quiet!"*
> *Shhhhhhh . . . ."*

QUESTIONS INVOLVING UNDERSTANDING = COMPREHENSION

Literal Comprehension Definition: This comprehension format demonstrates understanding facts presented in the story. Each question's answer may be found by recalling or rereading the story. For the "Sammy . . ." story, the are examples of Literal, then Applied and lasty Implied comprehension.

Examples of Literal Comprehension:

1. Who's the main character of the story?
2. Who was a friend of this main character?
3. What did Sammy want, and how did this make him feel by not having it?
4. Where is one place Sammy went to find what he wanted?
5. What is the last word in the story?

Applied Comprehension Definition: These types of questions find the reader not having the direct answer in the story, but rather the reader's reaction to the story. This may be done by comparison and contrasting one's own thoughts and feelings about it.

Examples of Applied Comprehension:

1. How do you feel concerning Sammy's reaction to noise? Do you have the same response, why or why not?

2. If someone came to you for assistance with a problem, how do you suppose you'd respond?
3. Buddy Bullfrog made some suggestions to help Sammy, would you do the same thing, and if not, what would you do?
4. Do you think Buddy Bullfrog's idea was good? Why or why not?
5. At the close of the story, how does Sammy feel and why do you think that?
6. What is your reaction to the noise around you?
7. Noise served as a stressor for Sammy and so he wanted quiet. What are two stressors you have, and why do you suppose you have these?
8. Whom would you go to for assistance in a stressful situation, and why do you suppose you would select that person or those people?
9. Sammy became involved in mindfulness, a period of reflection and quiet. What do you do to be mindful?

Implied Comprehension Definition: This is what's "inferred" in the story from what has been presented. The questions involve the reader or listener's reaction to what has been laid as the "groundwork" of the story. The questions require the use of context clues or observation of illustrations in a picture book. Also, this type of comprehension may result from oral, visual, tactile, or kinesthetic material presented in the book.

Examples of Implied Comprehension:

1. What do you suppose are the general natures of Sammy and his friend Buddy?
2. Do you think that the places these two characters visit and the people there are responsive to the request for quiet? Explain your answer.
3. Do you think that Buddy's initial reaction was based on what he'd want someone to do for him, and why do you or don't you think that?
4. Based on Sammy's asking Buddy for help, who else do you think Sammy would go to for assistance and why?
5. In the end of the story, is it implied that Sammy found what he was seeking?
6. What do you think are the two messages of this book?

DEFINING A THEMATIC CONTRASTING TOPIC

The addressing of the three types of comprehension in the preceding paragraphs with examples may be extended to asking types of contrasting applied comprehension questions. You're invited to take a moment and revisit the portion of the story presented and then the examples of Applied

Comprehension questions. For the former of these revisiting experiences, you'll note that Sammy didn't like the noise around him each day. The questions address one's own reaction or speculation about what one would do in a similar situation or how one would handle seeking help or give it. This is well and good because the answers require thinking that involves recall, reflection, speculation, problem solving, and risk-taking, which are metacognitive skills. Then there is evidenced comparing and contrasting and predicting, which involve the first and second phases of thinking skills. Now let's examine differing those questions, which reverse the book's theme.

EXAMPLES OF PERSONALIZING QUESTIONS USING APPLIED COMPREHENSION

These are questions that, when referring to this particular *Sammy Snail's* book, require a switch from the main topic of Sammy's stress to what things make the reader happy or provide a comfort zone. Examples include the following: (1) Sammy was bothered by the noise around him each day; what are things that make you happy each day? (2) How do you think you'd go about experiencing your day without distractions or things that annoyed you? Provide an example of one of these things. (3) To whom do you go for comfort, and why did you select that person? (4) De-stressing is a technique that requires your calming yourself or relaxing. It's the opposite of something that causes stress. What are situations that you find pleasurable and joyful? Why do you suppose they do?

OVERALL RESULTS OF COMPREHENSION QUESTIONS

For the most part this author suggests that using all three types of comprehension questions assists the reader in "knowing" the story. There is opportunity for character analysis by using fact-based questions. These answers, since they can be referenced in the story, bring immediate success for the student.

With respect to Applied Comprehension questions, the reader has the opportunity to use Basic Awareness, Critical and Creative Thinking, and Metacognitive Thinking skills. Realizing, comparing, and contrasting, sequencing story events, prioritizing, evaluating, initial and advanced deciding, recalling, reflecting, and self-actuating come with answering the questions posed. Doing this provides personal responses based on one's own life experiences as much as what happened in the story. And, when given the opportunity to share, one discovers how others in the class responded and allows for more speculation and possibly an altering of one's original opinion or thoughts, and ideas.

There is no right or wrong answer for Applied Comprehension, as these questions are based on one's personal reaction to the story and are usually opinion- or idea-based. Implied Comprehension allows the student to speculate on what will happen next. Also, these types of questions are ones that first are based on what happened in the story and what the reader thinks will happen next. Therefore, one uses extensive metacognitive skills with advanced deciding, evaluating, recalling, and basing an answer on one's life experiences.

JOINING THINKING, FEELING, MEMORY, AND COMPREHENSION

A culminating thought for this chapter is to link this one to the previous three chapters. In a manner of speaking, this linking has already been done. As at this or any given moment, you are joining these four topics in the previous chapters and this one. You may question, "How?" And that would be explained by requesting you to recognize the thought you are having at the present moment and how you feel, in an emotional or in a sensory manner. Then, be aware that how you feel relies on your past experiences, which include those presented in these chapters. You know what you're doing? You're using your *thinking, feelings*, and *memory,* to *comprehend/understand* each of these terms.

In the mental action of joining the topics of these first four chapters, you are realizing, prioritizing, sequencing, deciding about, comparing, and contrasting to others' reactions if there's sharing. Evaluating is evidenced when what you're thinking becomes self-actuation. You are taking action, in the present moment, with reflection making the connections with the first chapters in a natural reciprocal fashion. The entire time you used your memory of what these chapters related. And now you are asked to use the skills thus far provided when reading about a book or story involving plot and social-emotional learning(s).

Ultimately, as you read this book, you shall come to realize that each of these seven beginning chapters is part of each reading strategy. And the recognition comes so easily that you may not even know what cognition is happening, unless you truly examine what you're thinking and feeling, as well as what involved memory and comprehension to move forward in your acquisition of knowledge.

Chapter 5

The Plot

Sequence of a Story

STORY SEQUENCING

Do you remember the Preface regarding the past four chapters? If you do, then the last of the hierarchal listings was realizing a story's plot has distinct parts. These are now laid out for you and explained by stating what is in each. Then, just for the fun of it, there's a look back at chapter 3's *The First Bicycle Ride* story, as it's addressed by applying these following parts of a plot.

PLOT SEQUENCE

The chronological order elements of a story, whether it is a fictional novel, short story, a book about animals, sports, hobbies, nonfiction, or personal experiences, has this order of the plot:

1. *Exposition:* This portion of the plot addresses the characters and setting with the conflict as well.
2. *Rising Action:* This is where the conflict and building of reader suspense occurs.
3. *Climatic Moment:* This is when the conflict and tension reach a high point, and one makes a decision.
4. *Falling Action:* The decision is carved out as the conflict gets resolved and the story tension subsides.
5. *Resolution:* This is the closing point of the story's conflict. The problem is resolved or a solution to it has been reached.

Before providing a sample from chapter 3's story, think of a story you've read or told and see if you can identify the plot structure. Use your computer to record this structure, and then look at what follows.

Here's an example of the plot's chronological order in chapter 3's *The First Bicycle Ride*.

Exposition: The story was about the author's first time riding a bike. She was seven years old, and her dad was holding onto the back of the bicycle seat to assist his daughter's staying steady and being successful at this adventure.

The setting was in front of their house, in the street, and then on the sidewalk. There was information that as time went by, the main character rode her bike up the street to a friend's house and, for that matter, all around the neighborhood where she lived.

A conflict was introduced as to whether the girl would be able to ride her new bike or not.

Rising Action: The girl gets on her bike, and her dad holds onto the back of the seat. But the girl begins to peddle faster, making it difficult for the dad to run alongside the bike and hold onto the back of the seat to guide her.

Climatic Moment: The girl peddles so fast that her dad lets go of the bike. When realizing this, the girl doesn't steer well, and the handlebars wobble as she steers the bike off the street onto the curb and sidewalk.

Falling Action: The girl falls and cries, as her dad comes running to her side to see what happened/if she's okay. He asks what happened, and she states, "You let go." The father comforts his daughter.

Resolution: The girl explains that she wanted her dad to hold onto the bike. However, recovering from the experience, she goes on to ride the bike by herself, successfully.

CHAPTER QUESTIONS

1. What are the parts of a story plot? Is it good to have these in sequential order? Explain your answer.
2. Take a story you know from a children's book or elsewhere, and explain each of the five parts of the plot structure. Is doing this easy or difficult? Explain your answer.

Chapter 6

Character Counts with Social-Emotional Learning

CHARACTER

What better way to begin this chapter with the one thing everyone teaches regardless of one's job title. As you read in the Introduction, your character is on display wherever you go. You show it through the things you say and the actions you take. This is true for your students too. So, how do you, as an educator, help shape that character to bring about a classroom that experiences harmony and positive-based participation in the SEL realm?

Perhaps it's best to begin with a definition of "character" and know that it's first shaping takes place in the home and community before the student even attends school. This term, at its most basic level, is referred to as your "personality," which is synonymous with your behavior, disposition, temperament, and persona.

Your character is formed with input from all those involved in the school, as well as in social and emotional settings, because your personality is shaped by your reaction to those around you, which involves the three types of memory explained in chapter 3. Also, important is the integration of those memories into your demeanor or how you conduct yourself, which is shown on a regular basis.

In a classroom one's character is evidenced through actions and reactions to academic and social situations. What one thinks and feels comes into play to form that classroom community. So, you may question, "What is a community?" If memory serves me correctly, this is the way one exchanges information and shares within a setting . . . any setting. But what is shared is the basis for that community.

COMMUNITY

A group of people living in the same place having *particular characteristics (not interests)* in common, such as caring, sharing, and showing *"civility,"* which means being courteous and/or polite in behavior and/or speech.

> The best way to establish a community is to have communication with another or others. This requires a give and take; a back and forth, an engaged exchange of information, interests, ideas, thoughts, opinions, and feelings. (Schiering, 1999; 2015, 2017)

SEL: EXPLANATION

With the previous definitions in mind, you're asked to visualize a classroom setting where SEL is happening. What you'd likely see is conversational exchanges while working on an assignment, whether interactive or not. Or you might teach SEL by starting a conversation with your students. Having a conversation brings about social discourse, conversation with one another. This would be the "social" or "S" part of the acronym. Then, there'd be the "E" part which refers to managing one's feelings or emotional responses to stimuli. The "L" refers, of course, to learning about one's own ideas or those of classmates and the teacher or varied topics. It is the sharing that brings about SEL.

The exchanges in the aforementioned community setting for SEL would take place between students and the teacher as well. Hausfather, in 1996 commented, "Instead of a teacher dictating her meaning to students for future recitation, a teacher should *collaborate* with her students in order to create meaning in ways that students can make their own."

For social discourse, perhaps Vygotsky's 1978 suggestion should be recognized with focus on such things as self-control, demonstrating empathy, or at least concern for others' feelings. The conversations would be not just with class members but also with the teacher. Schiering adds in 1999 that these interactions would likely include the six international traits of a person of good character: being responsible, kind, fair, trustworthy, a good citizen, and respectful.

Teaching Good Character with SEL

Since we now know what SEL entails, let's take a look at the previously mentioned six good character traits. These adhere to the characteristics mentioned in the definition of the word "community," a few paragraphs previous to this one. In class, SEL would involve the identification of what each of the six international person-of-good character traits means to the students.

Ask for examples and provide the opportunity to work in small groups to define each of these (examples are the topic of chapter 14). Be aware that the last one is profound, as there are so many different types of exhibiting "respect." How is one to know which is being addressed if a definition is not provided? One would not know, and so it is the recording of what is meant by each character trait to help in one's exhibiting it. Of course, there is reinforcement offered with teacher modeling of respect, and creating scenarios where certain traits may be exhibited, and examined for clarity.

SIX INTERNATIONAL CHARACTER TRAITS OF A PERSON WITH GOOD CHARACTER

For the importance of character traits or development of SEL, teachers and students, students and students need to exchange information and have conversations about what constitutes a person of good character. But what should the topic be? How about the six international traits of a person of good character? These are about individual's being respectful, a trait which includes being caring, honest, courteous, compassionate, open-minded, accepting, and the list continues. See for yourself what you think these character traits represent.

Take a moment and jot down what you recognize as behavior representing respectfulness. Next, refer to chapter 14 that has anecdotes on the international traits regarding a time when each trait was exhibited by oneself, another person or persons. Use this activity not only to define the traits but relate to them through experiences the students have had with each trait. This exercise establishes classroom community through sharing with one another on positive happenings. Another thought is to project how one might notice when being a person of good character would be helpful and keep a log regarding those times. Be sure to note politeness and consideration with making positive statements. Prepare students for their success.

A Little More Information: Social Competence and Emotional Competence

Social competence includes one's ability to make positive contributions to the community and to cooperate with others. Emotional competence refers to one's ability to identify and understand one's emotions and how those can impact their thoughts, behaviors, and attitude. It involves the comprehension/understanding that emotions can be processed so one can remain calm, focused, and successful, even in the face of negativity (www.flyfivesel.org).

Author's Suggestion: Refer to Chapter 2 on Feelings for more clarification about emotional competence.

Teaching includes a constant exchange of information that involves the first five chapters of this book. Some of that exchange emphasizes skill building in academics and skill building in socialization. The two, from this author's perspective, are continually intertwined and form, for each academic area, the interactions that establish socializing. This skill building can be taught by having activities that include beliefs and values of the class members, as well as their common social and societal realities.

Practicing and Teaching Character, Community, and SEL

Later in this chapter is an activity titled "Getting Acquainted." That serves as a beginning for students to talk "with" each other. It's designed to have class members discover some characteristics of one another through acknowledgment of similarities and differences on relatively innocuous topics. This is a whole class activity and the beginning of teaching socialization for the students. While this activity isn't a deep understanding of classmates, it establishes the groundwork for socialization within the academic setting. From there the teacher may decide to teach many lessons about these "commonalities" the class experiences when getting acquainted.

COMMONALITIES

These commonalities are for sharing and are communal and collective. For teaching these involve social realities and include such things as favorite foods, sports, hobbies, gathering places, music interests, television series, programs, movies, games, fun activities, reflecting and sharing on what makes for a good time. This sharing provides opportunities to bring the class together with respect to interests. It's positive based and avoids negativity.

Then, beliefs and values can be addressed to truly get to know one another. While interests are interesting, it's one's beliefs and values that define one's character. It is here, at the core of who someone is, that brings a class of students together to form a community. And, this author believes that, in order for learning to be embraced, first must be that community where students feel safe, accepted, and appreciated by the teacher and classmates.

Beliefs: *This is your concept, involving thinking and feelings as to whether something is true, untrue, good, bad, or even exists.*

Values: *These involve beliefs as to whether something is right or wrong, or the level of importance something has based on one's experience.*

TEACHING ABOUT BELIEFS AND VALUES: AN IN-CLASS ACTIVITY

For the explicit development of a classroom community where best character traits may be shown there is an activity involving an individual's beliefs and values. This activity brings awareness, critical and creative thinking, and applies reflection, recall, analysis, and evaluation through self-actualizing practiced. The simple thing is that the students come to know one another on a personal basis, which addresses the core of who they are. The beliefs and values shared within the classroom environment encompass areas beyond that setting, as there is no limit to just academic, but not an emotional scope of one's character.

So, here's how this activity works: Separate the class into groups of five or six and give them time to discuss and reach consensus on five beliefs and five values they have. Then, bring the whole class together and, on a chart or Smart Board, or individual computers, if available, make a composite list of those beliefs and values recorded. Put a check next to any repetition from either list. Lastly, share on why the class thinks these were addressed and the level of importance of each value.

PRE-ACTIVITY: BELIEFS AND VALUES

The teacher makes a list of five beliefs and values thought to be important.

Belief and Values Activity List: Sources: NYS Project SAVE (2000–present) and N.Y.S Dignity for All Students Act Workshop (Schiering, 2013–present) September–December 2022:
Location: A University in NY, Ages of Participants: 19–35

ACTIVITY: BELIEFS AND VALUES

Starred beliefs relate that these were mentioned two to four times within and/ or between workshops.

Beliefs: Honesty is important*, everything happens for a reason*, being respectful*, happiness, safe*, kindness*, honesty, equality in schools, equal opportunity for everyone*, ourselves*, freedom*, kindness goes a long way, physical exercise, fairness*, agree to disagree*, help those in need, communication is key*, sports, everyone's voice matters*, son's little league team, good nutrition, pizza, karma, support communication skills*, no put down; only lift ups*.

Values: All of those listed were mentioned more than one time in any given workshop. Honesty, empathy, coffee, loyalty, fairness, integrity, politeness, friendship, loved ones, family, friends, peace, caring, being accepting, being a good listener, consideration, concern for others, being thoughtful, understanding, respect, empathy, trust, being responsible, courage, integrity, compassion, relationships, loyalty, education for all, freedom of speech, diversity embraced, equality, time, good health, opportunities, healthy life and work balance.

Post Activity: Compare your list of beliefs and values to those of your class. There is sometimes an awakening here in that different age groups have different beliefs and values or the priority of one is higher than another. Or there is a match regardless of age groups.

What this author has found is that whether compiling a list in Europe, the United States, or South America, the lists are primarily the same!

TEACHING ABOUT HOW NEGATIVELY IMPACTS ONE'S CHARACTER

Stress

Up to this point, this book has provided ideas and discussed SEL involving persons of good character. There is one major deterrent regarding being a person of good character, and that is STRESS!

From the spring of 1999 through January of 2022 this author has conducted, on a monthly basis, at Molloy University, 384 workshops addressing character. SEL, and teaching civility with ways to teach and bring about classroom and school harmony, a place where civility and community abide have also been mainstay topics. Add those presentations in several European countries, such as Denmark, Norway, Ireland, Iceland, England, Belgium, and Scotland, along with Columbia, South America, and the Republic of Georgia, the total workshops and conference presentations add up to well over 400.

These N.Y.S. workshops are titled DASA (Dignity for All Students Act) and Project SAVE (Safe Schools Against Violence in Education). The attendees were asked to compile a list of things that had caused them stress either during their childhood, teen, or adult years, inside or outside an educational institution. The list is as follows:

Death of a family member; Divorce, Parent/family vacation; Fear of or loss of job, or change in job status; Fear of abandonment, Moving to another geographic location; Making friends; Addition of another adult or sibling to the family; Supervisor or assistant change; Theft of personal possession; Parental and/or sibling relationships; Home arguments; Change in family financial condition; Fear of failure; dogs; Close friend sick or injured; Self-illness or injury; Change in financial situation; Unexpected pregnancy; Trouble with Grandparents; Fear of storms; Concern about car; home conditions; Regimentation at work or children responding to school poorly; Fear of teachers/supervisor; Bullying (for adults this is usually sarcasm expressed in the workplace); Being put down or not appreciated, Too many activities; No time to relax; Too much time, Boredom, family or relative/friend's alcohol or other substance abuse; Going away from comfort zone; Traveling or not traveling with others; Theft of personal item, Sibling rejection or dispute; Inability to cope; The pandemic, social distancing, having to wear a mask indoors, being back in face-to-face classes, your appearance, comparing yourself to others, academically, and socially, looks, personality, popularity, ability level, proving yourself, valuing you. and something not listed, but you think is tremendously stressful.

STRESS ACTIVITY

Instructions

Hmmm, that seems like a strange title for an activity. However, just as it's important to teach SEL with activities that bring about social discourse, it's also important to address what may thwart this. Poor or controversial behavior is a negative in a classroom. For example, bullying or disrespect. In fact, these activities are about recognizing that stress is a deterrent to being a person of good character because you are probably not representing your real self.

As with the Beliefs and Values activity, separate the class into groups of your choosing. Show the list of stressors, and have each group agree, reach consensus, on what are the five greatest stressors in their lives. Next, bring the class together and list these stressors so the group may see what most impacts those in the room on that day. Identify repetitions if there are any. Now, address what you, as the teacher, have come to realize are reasons for any of these stressors.

The big question is, "What caused these stressors?" After this author's research and listening to opinions of others in workshops given over twenty-three years, she identified four "reasons" that bring about that most uncomfortable stress. These are as follows (Schiering, 1999–present):

1. Change of routine, and this leads to,
2. Loss of one's sense of security, which likely brings about,
3. Fear of the unknown, which is, as stated by Zig Ziglar, "False evidence appearing real (https://www.ziglar.com Blog), and
4. Wanting, but not receiving acceptance, or acknowledgment of who we are, or an accomplishment.

When one examines these four, it is evident that the first three may happen sequentially or simultaneously. However, if the former, you're invited to take a look at the pandemic which caused a total change in people's routines with schools closing in many parts of America, and instruction done from home on computers. That change brought about a lessening of one's feeling of security, because of a fear of the unknown. The last reason for stress was more personal with not being recognized for our successes.

Teaching Classroom Skills for Good Character and SEL

It's important to know that being a person of good character, just like any other skill, occurs over time with practice. Opportunities need to be provided to practice these learned reactions to situations. Reflecting, synthesizing, and analyzing the information help develop one's good character. Role-playing, and in-class discussions, may assist in providing scenarios where behaviors may be demonstrated that represent the aforementioned six international character traits. The following suggestions for conduct may well provide discussion material for teaching SEL. Also, of importance is to explain such terms as courtesy and examples of uplifting statements. For that matter see how many might be suggested and put them on a wall display.

Suggestion: Provide ideas for future positive actions or reinforcement of present ones. Make notes of these in a journal and/or have a discussion with another or a class if you're teaching.

Teaching Social and Character Skills: Home, Community, School

The most important component of teaching others to be people of good character and how it counts/matters, as well as teaching SEL, involves modeling. That word, "model," has been bandied about quite a bit and so here's an example for teaching such a character trait with one's social-emotional involvement.

SCENARIO: PARENT AND FIVE-YEAR-OLD CHILD

The child has fallen and scraped her knee. She is crying, and the dad notices this. He comes forward offering words of caring and kindness, such as, "I see you scraped your knee. I know this must hurt a lot. Let me help you up, and we'll clean it off and put on a bandage where the scrape is. I have scraped my knee, so I know how it hurts and that the pain will go away, shortly. In the meantime, let me help you. I love you."

The parent has modeled caring, and the child has been a witness to this with her dad's kind and thoughtful words, and actions. When she sees someone in a similar situation, the memory comes forward, and the child will likely practice the same response, thus exhibiting caring and concern.

Disclaimer

As an educator, parent, or authority figure, possibly even a friend, I cannot teach you to care for another. I may model it, and explain it in a scenario, as in the previous example. But, getting you to care is not necessarily learned, as there needs to be something within a person to experience this action. However, if seen repeatedly, showing caring may be copied and evidenced, just not necessarily owned. Can you feel caring inside you?

This caring situation is a conundrum, to say the least. However, over time, that this may be developed and displayed. Or it may be displayed without inner social emotional attachment. Still, not to teach what good character through modeling or explaining and demonstrating SEL would be far greater a loss for creating a viable classroom community. Subsequently, you should keep in mind that Character Counts strategies and SEL are necessary modeling components in one's home, classroom, school, and community, or wherever you happen to be.

Good Character and SEL Modeling Examples

Demonstrate courtesy, admit your mistakes and seek to correct them, give uplifting statements when conversing, have a daily sharing time, be an active listener (this means talking with another or others), ***be nice to yourself, pay attention when another person is speaking, collaborate, share, cooperate by preventing scapegoating (blaming someone for something, as opposed to taking responsibility), refrain from pitting one person against another, model the six international traits of a person of good character, make guiding statements, emphasize good sportsmanship, create opportunities to work together, model and promote kindness through appropriate language, lead by example, talk about the need to care for all living things, and regularly share 'What's the right thing to do?' (Schiering, 1999–present)

FIRST THINGS FIRST: BEGINNING CLASSROOM COMMUNITY

SEL: A GETTING ACQUAINTED CLASSROOM ACTIVITY

Pretend it's the start of a school year or perhaps the start of a new semester, or, really, any time of the school year when addressing *SEL* is desired. One of the first things a teacher wants to do is bring the class participants together. Why? This activity is so we can realize similarities or differences in an innocuous manner and cause the atmosphere in the classroom to be pleasant and warm. To create that "safe" space, the following activity sheet was designed, to achieve that result. And it also seeks to establish a SEL situation by establishing the classroom setting as a comfort zone.

And after this initial get together, feel free to repeat getting further acquainted a few weeks later, or every month. The questions may remain the same, or you may use your own; a class-contributed ones are a suggestion.

"A plain and simple truth for this book's author is that you will have learning going on only if the classroom participants feel at ease in that shared environment" (Schiering, a long time ago, when she started teaching in Ohio). That concept is a key factor in every class at any grade level from beginning school years to postgraduate ones. It's the initial building block for SEL. Happy space, happy place, and grace.

Activity Sheet Directions

Mill around the classroom with the question sheet provided you and find different people to answer the questions. Try not to cluster into groups but remain with one to two people at most to get the answers to the sheet's questions. Record the names of those giving the answers on your paper. Feel free to use a nearby desktop to secure the question paper or place a book under the sheet so you'll have ease in recording responses. Follow-up activities may take a few days to complete and appear after students complete the following questionnaire:

Activity Sheet Questions

1. What's your name? _____
2. Find someone who likes to read the same genre of books you read, and record the genre and person's name. (List on the board in the front of the room book genres with illustrations of each genre. Children's picture book = "Cat in the Hat.")
    a. Book Genre _____
    b. Person or person's name _____
3. Locate a person who has a pet at home.
    a. Type of pet and its name_____
    b. Person's name _____
4. Locate a person who has nearly the same hand size as you.
    a. Hand size in inches_____
    b. Person's name_____
5. Locate a person who has the same or nearly the same number of siblings as you.
    a. Number of siblings, and if none then record, zero _____
    b. Person's name _____

6. Locate the person who has traveled the greatest distance away from the state in which you reside.
   a. Name of the state and distance from here_____
   _____
   b. Person's name_____
   ____
7. Locate a person with the same or nearly the same number of letters in the first name.
   a. Number of letters_____
   b. Person's name _____
8. Locate a person who has a favorite sport similar to your own or just has a favorite sport that's not the same as yours..
   a. Name of the sport and same or not_____
   _____
   b. Person's name_____
9. Locate a person who has a similar favorite food as you have.
   a. Name of the food _____
   b. Person's name _____
10. Locate a person who has a similar favorite color as you have
    a. Name of color_____
    b. Person's name _____

On the lines provided below, state your personal answer to the three questions and then find a classmate with whom you can share these responses:

1. *What do you think is important about this year in school and why?*
   _____
   _____
   _____

2. *State one idea about what you think it means to be a person who is respectful.*
   _____
   _____
   _____

3. *What are your thoughts on how and why an individual's understanding of classroom community impacts their learning?*
   _____
   _____
   _____

Author's Note: This "Getting Acquainted" activity is not a "stand-alone" one. There are follow throughs or follow-ups for everyone. What comes next are some ideas for extending the first time you use this unifying classroom tactic.

Follow-up Activity #1

Go around the classroom and find those who answered each question on your paper. See if you can identify that person and their answer.

Follow-up Activity #2

Share with the whole class, when called upon, your name, then go through each question and identify the name of the person(s) from whom you received answers. Be sure to provide the given answer that you recorded. Classmates may assist you in getting the right answer.

Follow-up Activity #3

Make a classroom or personal chart of the questions and answers, and post these on the side of your desk (depending on grade level) for later reference by you or classmates. If you're in high school or middle school, then simply make the chart and put it in a place for safe-keeping.

Follow-up Activity #4

Test your memory: Whom can you identify by name in our classroom, and what are three things that you know about that person? Go over and nicely greet your classmates each day, as you get more and more acquainted. And remember, the more you know about your classmates, the greater the understanding and forming of friendships.

A Few "Keep-in-Mind" Closing Concepts for This Chapter

- You can change any situation from unpleasant to pleasant by an act of your conscious will! Please rely on yourself to do this and not someone else, because ultimately, you must rely on you.
- "You can give to another only that which you first have for yourself. Just as you can give someone a pencil because you have it, so too can you give character traits, because you have them" (Schiering, S. 1998, 2017, 2020).
- "No put downs . . . only lift ups! This point includes being that way with yourself" (Schiering, 1976).
- "Our life is not about forgetting but forgiving. This can be read and said, "Our life is not about for getting, but for giving" (Million, 1990/2017).
- "Use a student-centered approach when teaching. And make your classroom as interactive as possible with students' auditory, visual, tactile and kinesthetic engagement in learning."

- "If you act badly that doesn't mean I have to copy your behavior. Not copying poor behavior is an act of one's conscious will. Basically, you determine how you behave and whether you are a person of good character" (Schiering, 1967).
- "There are 'trigger' words that very well may impact adverse behaviors. The trigger for me is the word 'disappointed.' A sentence with this word is, 'I am disappointed in you' (Schiering, 1999-present). Using trigger words may possibly unleash poor behavior and resentment towards the deliverer of such words. Best to be positive and compliment a person on things well done than diminish a person with negative comments. My mother used to put it this way: 'You'll get more with sugar than with salt and feel better about yourself in the process'" (Schiff-After, 1953).
- "Preparing your students for success may be evidenced in the way you word things. Instead of saying, 'You failed this test. Didn't you study?' say, 'Let me assist you with this topic'."
- "Realize that not everyone does well on written tests. Make accommodation. One of these may be giving the test orally to those who are better with the auditory modality."
- "Wherever you go, instead of saying to yourself 'what's in this for me', or 'What am I getting from this?' . . . say WHAT MAY I GIVE TO THIS EXPERIENCE" (Schiering, 1999–present).

CHAPTER QUESTIONS

1. What is the main topic of this chapter?
2. What are some thoughts and feelings you have about this chapter?
3. How do you think this chapter connects to teaching reading? Explain your answer.
4. What are the techniques you could use to promote SEL?
5. Do you see yourself using the Getting Acquainted activity? Why or why not?
6. What are three "Closing Concepts" you think to be most important in this chapter, and why did you select these?

PART II

TEACHING READING STRATEGIES PRELUDE

Chapter 7

Guidelines

Oral Reading Presentations and Silent Reading Directives

INTRODUCTION

The previous chapters in part I of this book has dealt with preparing one for reading and/or intertwining oral reading and silent reading. This author has addressed thinking/cognition, feelings, memory, comprehension/understanding, and character counts with SEL. This chapter commences Part II of this book and begins with some guides for oral presentations of reading material on a specified topic and then silent reading watchpoints. These presentations are designed to help you as much as your students. Some are given for you to review.

ORAL READING AND/OR ORAL PRESENTATION SUGGESTIONS

1. Be engaging.
2. Provide an energetic style of delivery.
3. Involve the participants through discussion or activities.
4. When possible, record class sharing on topics addressed.
5. Have a pleasant demeanor.
6. Create a community of positivity by modeling positivity.
7. Show interest in participants.
8. Have opportunities for interaction.
9. Be consistent with opportunities for participation.
10. Allow for different forms of communication with cooperation and/or collaboration. Examples include small groups, individual, partnership, collaboration, and/or cooperation.
11. Be positive and uplifting.

12. Be agreeable when opinions vary from your own.
13. Allow time for questions.
14. Being agreeable and allowing time for Questions and Answers. Be accepting.
15. Being accepting and sincere.

ORAL READING PRESENTATION EXAMPLES

"What is your personal comment regarding the 15 'Presentation Suggestions' for an Oral reading? Write your opinions in a journal or have a discussion with someone who looked at these suggestions. Once you've responded you're invited to read on and look at responses to those 15 suggestions. These came from attendees (teacher candidates or teachers, administrators, and school personnel) at this author's Preventing School Violence or Dignity for All Students Act (DASA) workshops, which are mandated by New York State for teacher certification (Instructor: M. Schiering, 1999–present). These workshops are sponsored by Molloy University's Continuing Education School. These responses were collected over a 24- and 11-year time span, respectively. No names were attached to the examples, which were given by several hundred people with these representing the most frequent responses.

1. *Being engaging*: Engaging and involving the audience so we weren't just sitting there for so many hours. We were continually actively involved.
2. *Providing an energetic style of delivery*: The delivery style was exciting, and "storytelling" was a technique used to involve us. The stories were personal experiences that the instructor had on the topics. An example would be how "fear" might cripple someone's thinking, such as going on a roller coaster ride as a child. (That was my favorite story.) Because of her experience she later on did not want her children to go on the ride. Not that she didn't let them, but she attempted to hold them back from the experience by not going to amusement parks.
3. *Involving the participants*: Strategies included small-group work and partnerships, creative poster making, reading to others, and graphing.
4. *Recording class sharing on topics addressed*: We recorded varied ideas on charts for our present and future reference. We took pictures of these charts. An example was what we, as a group of strangers, when meeting in groups wrote down what we considered to be our beliefs and values. These we then shared, with each group sending a representative to write the group's responses on wall-mounted chart paper. Everyone

got to see what bound us together. Most importantly, all showed respect for our thoughts.
5. *Having a pleasant demeanor*: *Modeling civility:* The instructor set the tone for this course through her pleasant and uplifting demeanor. Ideas shared were not rejected, but rather accepted.
6. *Creating a community*: We didn't know each other. Some people were from states other than New York. Right from the beginning we had a *Getting Acquainted* activity that involved talking with one another. We came together as a group through our sharing.
7. *Emphasizing self-awareness and care*: We emphasized caring first for oneself so you may care for others. Also, we accentuated the importance of good mental health.
8. *Being real*: *in the present:* We made connections to real-life situations when civility was in-practice and when it wasn't. We shared feelings and thoughts too as to the level of importance of civility and ways to prevent school violence.
9. *Being genuine and showing interest:* Energy was palpable. We were involved through active listening and discussion because this is exactly what the instructor did. We utilized the example of talking with others.
10. *Having examples of interaction:* The entire workshop was interactive. One activity I liked best was when we read a picture book to our partner. The professor provided the books and these were about ethical issues and moral ones too. We recorded, on large chart paper that was pinned to the wall, the book title and message so we could see people's interpretations and reactions to the books.

    This activity was fun and very informative. I can use this technique in my fifth-grade classroom. I think this book reading would work at any grade level;
11. *Providing consistent participation:* We used strategies that involved every person presenting, and we constantly emphasized participation in small- or whole-group formats, and partnerships too. I never got bored.
12. *Allowing for different forms of communication:* We had a texting time where we wrote something that we liked about someone. This activity could be done every day and not just in the workshop. I'd never been in a mandated course where we got to use social media, and using it was fun. The *after-sharing* was really good with so many different responses;
13. *Being positive and uplifting:* Everything we discussed focused on being positive. A beginning activity I'm going to use in my tenth-grade classroom was called *Hurts on the Heart*, and we got to see how put-down statements were upsetting. No matter how many lift-ups there are, these don't take away the hurt. Great visual. [Author's Note: This

activity is part of social-emotional learning and is in one of the lesson plans in part II of this book.]

A brief explanation of the Hurts on the Heart activity follows. A cutout paper heart with everyone's name on it is shown to the assemblage. Each is asked to give a put-down statement that someone might give to another person. An example would be, "You're stupid." The instructor explained that these statements would not be taken personally. Each statement called for the instructor to fold the paper with lines, upon completion, through everyone's name.

Then, each person made a positive statement, which the instructor took personally. An example would be, "You are my friend." Each statement called for the unfolding of one portion of the paper heart until it was fully unfolded. What the class saw was lines through every name and sometime more than one line. These were referred to as Hurts or Scars on the Heart.

The instructor explained that, even if a hundred more lift-up statements were given, these would not remove the hurts. Some hurts or scars last a few years, and some a lifetime. This depends on who is delivering the negativity. If it's someone for whom you care, the hurt lasts a long time.

14. ***Being agreeable and allowing time for Questions and Answers:*** Our ideas were taken-in, and if there was one that seemed questionable, it was questioned in a friendly way by asking for more explanation. The big thing was that we shared, openly, without fear of being put-down. Some people shared less than others in the big group, but it wasn't a big deal. We had several times for asking questions, and not just the instructor answered, but also people in the group gave their opinions.
15. ***Being accepting and sincere:*** The instructor and others here refrained from rejecting responses of those here. They accepted the exchange of ideas. Sometimes notes were taken to use later in one's classroom or future classroom. It was obvious the instructor was passionate about preventing school violence through civility (DASA) training, and for us to be involved in it back at our own classrooms, homes, or when with others.

Author's Note: Perhaps there is one final imperative for the teacher. This author saw it on a plaque she purchased and exhibits in the front of the room at every workshop she is asked to present. The sign reads:

We can't help everyone, but everyone can help someone.

Oral Reading Presentation Evaluation Criteria

Directions: After each of the nine "Criteria," place a score you think appropriate on a scale of 1–10. Ten is the highest score possible, Then, follow this with a general comment on your personal reaction to the presentation or oral reading. Using reflection, determine how your thoughts comments could apply to helping students' learning experiences.

1. Introduction
2. Presentation style (formal or informal)
3. Sequence
4. Voice-modulation
5. Stress and juncture
6. Consistence of presentation
7. Posture
8. Questions, if applicable
9. Closure

Silent Reading Suggestions

1. Be aware of the main idea of the story. What is the topic?
2. Know the names of the story characters and be able to describe them by their physical appearance and emotional treats ones as well.
3. Recognize the physical setting of the story and, if possible, the time of year or day when the story takes place.
4. Realize that each story has a particular mood or moods. Record what these are, and give an example of how they are verified in the story.
5. List at least five major events of the story in sequential order.
6. Realize the overall problem in the story.
7. Recognize the story solution and how this happened if there is a conflict in the story, or a decision to be made.

What's Next

First there is the explanation of what's contained in each Reading Strategy chapter. Then there are the six different reading strategies. Specifically, the six chapters, following chapter 8, have a definitive reading strategy that is described in detail. Then, there is for whom the strategy is best suited and why that is the case. Next, is a lesson plan with Motivation, Objectives, Activities, Questions for each activity, Differentiation of Instruction, and an Activity to extend the lesson. Additionally, there is a social-emotional learning activity aside from the lesson itself. This is specifically designed to be engaging.

We're Not the Same

We know that not everyone learns the same way. Just as we look different, we have ways of learning to read that are not in alignment with everyone else at the same grade or age level. Therefore, comprehension is varied in accordance with the reading strategy and one's reaction to it. *It is important to see that learning to read, regardless of one's age, is likely done differently from another person's way of accomplishing this.* What works for you may not work for someone else. Therefore, why the next chapters in this book relate various reading strategies is because not everyone learns the same way.

CHAPTER QUESTIONS

1. What do you think are the three most important components of an oral presentation? Explain why you selected these.
2. What are two silent reading suggestions and why do you think these to be important?
3. In the upcoming six chapters, reading strategies are examined. Why would one strategy be used as opposed to another be most helpful? Explain your answer.

Chapter 8

Content of Chapters 9–14 with Explanations

A CONTENT OVERVIEW

This book has already presented ideas for oral presentations including reading and silent reading guidelines. Now, this author delves into the Reading Strategies section with explanations about six different reading methods that address such things as (1) a description of the strategy, which includes, (2) whom it's best suited for with respect to using it in the teaching of reading, as well as (3) What's involved in teaching the reading strategy, and (4) Why it is appropriate respective of students' strengths and aiding in learning.

Addressing individuals as learners with an explanation of processing style and perceptual preferences being included in the strategy is given attention. Next, in each chapter, there is the presentation of a reading strategy lesson plan. The components of the lesson plan are explained after the purposes of the lesson plan, which follows this paragraph.

THE PURPOSES OF LESSON PLANNING

Why do you suppose divisions, schools, or departments of education at colleges and universities teach lesson plan writing? Hmm, the most succinct reason is to prepare you for teaching lessons at the grade level you're assigned. The lesson plans at college are to expose you to the experience of the scope and sequence of teaching the components of a designated topic in the classroom.

Lesson plans allow for a series of activities to "bring home" what is to be taught. Simultaneously, knowing how to write a lesson plan allows for you to rely on your ability (self-efficacy) through personal empowerment regarding knowledge on the requirements of planning what's to be covered/addressed in the curriculum.

The truth, as this author has seen it, is that teachers will likely, when actually teaching in the classroom, never, or rarely use the extreme detail of a higher education institute's requirements for designing a plan for each subject area. This point would be with respect to any lesson during any given day in one's classroom. *However, the detail and pattern you experience in learning to construct a lesson plan will be engrained in your brain.* Yes, that process, product, and content will exist in your taking action and implementing instruction in any subject area. However, for this book that subject area is exclusive to reading strategies and the detail is provided to serve as the means for future instruction at any grade level.

Some other purposes for the written lesson plan, as presented in reading strategy chapters 9–14 in this book, are assistance in future teaching, so the selection of the best reading strategies are available to you. This lesson plan devoted to a specific reading strategy may be for later demonstration as much as using different strategies to meet students' processing style. This also includes perceptual preferences (auditory, visual, tactile, and kinesthetic).

The lesson plans show you the "how to" of delivering information and includes interactive methods and technology, should it be available to you as a conduit for experiential learning. Then there are questions attached to each activity to stimulate class participation, as well as develop one's cognition and meta-cognition. Knowing how to teach a particular strategy with all those presented gives one the opportunity to compare these, as well as examine and analyze strategies best suited to the students' needs.

Lesson Plan Contents

Objective(s): The first portion of the lesson plan, as you may suppose, has the objective or objectives of the lesson. You present here what you want the students to learn. Naturally, these are in accordance with the strategy. And the objectives refer to the use of reading and/or ELA. Scope and sequence may be observed here, but that is most obvious in the "Activities" section. The grade level for whom the lesson is appropriate is also stated for your awareness of what group most benefits from the specified lesson.

Motivational Techniques: These are means of stimulating student interest in the lesson to be presented. For elementary students, these motivational strategies usually involve some sort of physical activity or ones a multi-modality approach. Still, a song or role-play may work for any age or grade level. Knowing students' interests assists in the writing of this section. Conversations, debates, storytelling, and discussions are also techniques to be considered prior to the actual activities of the lesson plan.

Activities with Accompanying Comprehension Questions: This section begins each activity with the words, "The students will." There may be a variation that reads, "After the teacher _____, the students will be able to . . ." Or there may be the phrase, "Following the reading of or naming some activity, the students will be able to . . . ." Something is stated so the students will be able to have knowledge prior to engaging in the activity. Key to this section is that it contains the (1) Content, (2) Process, and (3) Product of the lesson. In more detail that means (1) what's in the lesson, (2) activities to achieve learning goals, and (3) the end-product the students will produce.

The questions for each activity should number between 4 and 6. Put these in italics and parentheses after stating what the students will be able to do. The questions are specifically designed to stimulate students' thinking about the reading material or reading topic. Each question is to be a literal, applied, or implied comprehension question. Please see chapter 4 in part I of this book. The three different types of Comprehension Questions are defined and exemplified there. These types of questions are defined again in this chapter with different examples provided for each one.

Primarily, since literal comprehension relies on reading the book and extrapolating exact information from it, you, as the teacher, want to focus on applied and implied comprehension questions. However, it is good to begin with "literal" comprehension, as these are easily answered. The other two types of comprehension call for student engagement in thinking with a response of thoughts, ideas, opinions, judgments, or feelings.

The *applied* and *implied* questions address such skills as: analyzing, evaluating, comparing, contrasting, prioritizing, decision-making, generalizing, sequencing, classifying, organizing, and risk-taking. Please use the Hierarchal and Reciprocal Thinking Chart (figure 1.1) from chapter 1, step 1 to view and then examine the application of thinking skills through the use of varied comprehension questions.

LESSON PLAN: THREE TYPES OF COMPREHENSION QUESTIONS WITH EXAMPLES

1. Literal: These are fact-based types of comprehension. *(Who was the first USA president?)*. Answer: George Washington, as stated in the USA president's book.
2. Applied: These are adapting the questions to your point of view. *(If you were going to be a president of an organization, what one would you choose and why?)*. Possible answer: I'd like to be president of the school's student newspaper. I'd like this because I enjoy writing and editing.
3. Implied: These call for speculation about what will happen next, because of what has already been presented. The information is not

directly stated but leads the reader to think of what is happening or may happen in the flow of the story. It is similar to indirect evidence in science. *(When seeing bird footprints on the sand, but not seeing any birds, what do you think is implied?).* I would think that, after the rain, there were a lot of birds on the sand, because the footprints are of birds.

LESSON PLAN: DIFFERENTIATION OF INSTRUCTION: EXPLANATION AND WHY

"What do you suppose it means to differentiate a portion of a lesson? To get your answer, let's look at the definition which states that to differentiate means to distinguish and/or set apart. Set apart, from what, you may ask? In designing a lesson, it separates this section from the activities and all other parts of the lesson plan by having it stand alone.

As this author stated in 2011, "Differentiated activities adhere to the theme and general objective of the lesson, as the activities you design would not be repeated elsewhere in the lesson. Differentiating a portion of the lesson plan is for the entire class or several groups of students and not just one student with a specific problem . . . that's an adaptation. Differentiation is specifically applied to learners who would most benefit from this type of instruction."

TYPES OF DIFFERENTIATION: CONTENT, PROCESS, PRODUCT (SCHIERING, 2011)

1. *Learning by Pace* involves time on task that best accommodates learners. For advanced learners, writing a poem will take ten minutes. For those who may have some difficulty with writing a poem, fifteen to thirty minutes for this task will be provided.
2. *Learning by Ability Level* takes into consideration the general expectation of student performances at a given grade and/or age. The students are separated for the task of the lesson with notation of those who are advanced, average, or below average learners.
3. *Kinds of Instruction* refers to instructional techniques or methods. Passive recipients of knowledge would be diametrically opposed to the instructional strategy in which students are actively engaged in acquiring information. Subsequently, there may be interactive lessons, small-group or partnerships put into practice, or writing, role-play, creating slides, conducting an interview, to name a few kinds of instruction.
4. *Learners' Interests* includes such things as conducting research, creating an educational game, doing reporting with a mock interview, doing

a videotape, or constructing an illustrated slideshow. All of these would be options when addressing the same topic of a lesson.
5. *Learners' Needs* involves a subjective or objective evaluation component regarding instruction. The first of these is based on feelings or emotional reactions of students. The latter is focused on comparing and contrasting students' performances on, customarily, assessment. Students' needs vary as much as individuals themselves at any given time.
6. "*Processing Styles* addresses the emotional, sociological, psychological, and physiological preferences of students. Perceptual preferences may also be taken into consideration." (Dunn and Blake, 2008)
7. *Tier Lessons* involves instruction in which the assignment begins at a basic level and builds in complexity. "In this author's opinion, excellent cognitive skill application and comprehension are evidenced with Tier lessons, as there's a hierarchy established with regard to the increasing complexity of the tiers."

LESSON PLAN: DIFFERENTIATION OF INSTRUCTION IN CHARACTER DEVELOPMENT AND SOCIAL-EMOTIONAL LEARNING (SEL)

This section of the Lesson Plan relies on student interaction with emphasis on the positives of one's personality. Additionally, this section involves creating a safe and welcoming classroom-shared environment. Character Development or Character Counts relies on building one's self-image to recognize what's good about each member of the classroom. Teachers model appropriate behavior and encourage one's being enough. This is in opposition to comparing oneself to others or another and finding oneself to be less than, as opposed to just "different from" this person or these persons.

SEL involves students having conversations with one another on a variety of topics. Character traits would serve as an example. The key element in SEL involves exhibiting and applying the use of communication skills whereby there is an inclusive classroom. This is defined as a place where individuals are accepting of one another, regardless of their academic ability level. Also, there is omission of categorizing persons by other criteria, such as age or what are considered stereotypical components of one's physical features or cultural mores.

Lesson Extension: These are activities that extend the objectives of a lesson. In one of these, addressing knowing the capital of each state in the United States, have the students make a set of Task Cards. One side of the card would have the name of the state and its capital on the other. Each card is cut in half in a different shape so the match can be made by seeing the same shapes. This is a self-corrective activity. The students can make a pile of missed state capitals and then redo/repeat using these later to assist in learning the states and their capitals.

Assessment: This may be anything from a short answer-fill-in-the-blank, to multiple choice, to an essay/formal evaluation, to an informal observation of students' work. Some ideas for informal assessment include individual, small group, or whole class assignments: Task Cards, Picture Drawing, Timeline, Flash Cards, Electro-board, Flip Chute Cards, and/or Bulletin Board Construction. In the division of the class into groups to make Task Cards of vocabulary and matching definition, each group receives a list of ten words different from the other groups for word on one side and definition on the other side. Then, put the cards, all mixed-up, on the floor and have a whole class kinesthetic activity of putting the cards together.

LESSON PLAN: TEACHER AND STUDENT EVALUATIONS/ASSESSMENT: GUIDELINE

When one thinks of assessing students' work or knowledge of material taught, one thinks of a test. This may not be the case but may involve one of the formats mentioned in the previous paragraph. Regardless, there is one very important factor when assessing, and that is to emphasize the positives of students' work. How this may be done is relatively easy. Be sure to have yourself and students, when evaluating aloud or on paper, make "plus-type" comments. This goes with the philosophy of "No put downs . . . Only Lift ups."

Students want to feel good in their classroom. Teachers should want to have students feel good in the classroom. Therefore, accentuating the positive and deemphasizing the negatives are important for harmony, safety, and comfort in the learning environment.

One way of accomplishing this is to have students evaluate or assess other students' work, such as following a presentation of a project, making only statements about what they liked.

1. *Good Example:* The way you showed the different parts of an ecosystem, I thought, was really good with the illustrations you had and the three-dimensional figures as well.
2. *No, no:* If I had done this report/project, I would have used larger illustrations and made some three-dimensional. Why a *No, no*: Those presenting have spent time on their project and to refer to what might have been done when seeing what is done is deconstructive. Having a would-of, should-of, or could-of is not constructive, but fault finding and demeaning. Doing this is an overt exhibition of disappointment in what was presented. How does that help anyone? Certainly, the presentation is not going to be changed, as it was just delivered.

3. *The Term: Constructive Criticism:* Ah, you may be thinking that it's important to build-up (Construct) and to tear-down (criticize), but when assessing a person's or persons' work, that process may not be beneficial. Why? That's because people, in general, emphasize or dwell on the negatives, as opposed to the positives of what is said to oneself or others. Why? It's human nature. However, when you have *constructive criticism* the focus for the one receiving it is to dwell on the criticism part. Such focusing is not beneficial to realizing the positives or the constructive part of the evaluative statements/comments.

When the teacher and fellow students are praising others, then a feeling of comfort and things being "okay" persists. Trust develops, and a sense of well-being is established. For my years as an educator, I have continually practiced the idea of being positive, and, if there's a problem, then finding another way to teach the material. Or I speak privately to the student and ask for suggestions as to how the assignment may be done differently. This approach establishes collaboration and the sense of the student having a "say" in what's to be done. Positivity begets positivity. Talking "with" others or another begets joining for a common good.

THREE EXAMPLES OF CHANGING AN ASSIGNMENT TO MEET A STUDENT'S NEEDS

1. Tim, a fifth-grade student, was continually doing very well in class participation on nearly any topic that was presented as part of the class curriculum. However, when Tim took a multiple-choice, fill-in-the-blank, or matching test, he continually failed. So, one day this teacher asked Tim to stay a little bit during lunch. She read him the text questions and provided the possible answers or asked him for an answer. The result was a score of 100 percent on the test or close to 100 percent.

    What had happened was that the teacher changed to a mode of delivery to meet his strength in auditory processing. The result was Tim's, success. Personally, this author believes that *when you have one success, you seek another. When you have failure, you tend to get stuck in a place of discomfort and see yourself as a failure. There's no need for that if one uses a pro-active approach with respect to teach the way a student learns.*

2. The teacher graded the tests by putting a small green dot next to incorrect answers and a large "C" next to correct ones. Students looking over the shoulder of a classmate saw the "C's" and not the dots. With the positive approach, the student grew in strength and self-confidence when learning the material.

3. Reading aloud in a sixth grade class. Susan, since elementary school, had exhibited difficulty reading aloud from a book when called upon to do so. The teacher, realizing this problem, called Susan aside one day and informed her that, in two days, the class would read aloud. She'd like Susan to practice the four paragraphs on page 53 for that upcoming day's reading.

   She explained that Susan could practice at home, or the teacher would set aside some time for her to practice in their classroom. On the day of the reading, Susan was told that the teacher would call on her for those paragraphs. The result was that Susan practiced, and when called upon, read well. Classmates were impressed, and Susan felt a sense of acceptance. What happened was that Susan, over time, practiced all the pages to be read and was well prepared to do this in the classroom.

WHY USE DIFFERENT READING STRATEGIES?

We know that not everyone learns the same way. Just as we look different, we have ways of learning to read that are not in alignment with everyone else at the same grade or age level. Therefore, comprehension varied with the reading strategy and one's reaction to it. *It is important to visualize that learning to read as individuals, regardless of one's age, is, in all likelihood, done differently from another person's way.* It's the idea of what works for you may not work for someone else. Or, what works for me may not work for you. Therefore, as the next chapters in this book relate six different reading strategies, I reiterate that the reason for presenting these is because not everyone learns the same way.

Part III

TEACHING DIFFERENT READING STRATEGIES

Chapter 9

The Reciprocal Reading Strategy

STRATEGY EXPLANATION

Reciprocal Reading (RR) is an instructional strategy where the roles of teacher and learner are easily and continually interchanged or intertwined. Why, you may question, and that would be because the strategy is designed for cooperative group work. This means, as you likely know, that each member of the group has a specific responsibility within that setting. This approach is not much different from a team sport where each member has a specific thing to do. In baseball, for example, the pitchers, outfielders, short stop all have different responsibilities. Each responsibility requires the sharing and exchange of information so the sport can be played. That's the same for the four RR roles. Each one may be used by one group member each during a reading lesson, and then these would be switched during another one. Subsequently, there's a back and forth with knowing what's to be done and sharing responsibilities.

This discussion-style method assists in learners' active involvement while incorporating self-monitoring of what they read. Subsequently, one relies on one's ability to conduct a particular role while relying on other group members to do their assigned part. Another huge plus with using the RR strategy is that the reader/each group member comes to be involved in self-efficacy. What is that, you may wonder, and it's best explained by an individual's belief in their ability to do a specified task or exhibit a particular behavior. In a manner of speaking, self-efficacy is one's belief in oneself. It conveys an attitude of "I can do this!"

THE RECIPROCAL READING (R.R.) ROLES

The aforementioned roles revolve around a group of four persons with each being either a (1) Predictor, (2) Questioner, (3) Clarifier, or (4) Summarizer. These are defined as follows:

1. The predictor makes statements that address the theme, plot, characters, events, as much as story problem/solution, and particulars like the setting(s) of the story with what may happen. Illustrations, if present, may also be used to ask about what happens next. Or, information from the reading book or story is there to formulate ideas regarding the flow of the story, even the ending.
2. The Questioner role/person is the one who asks questions for the purpose of directing these to assist in comprehension of the story being addressed. The hierarchical and/or reciprocal thinking skills involved are those of asking questions to make comparisons of setting, characters, ideas presented, or the flow of the story, realizing the story topic, or prioritizing events or settings for sequencing, noting the impact of decisions, inciting moments, climatic section, with analyzing these or evaluating them.
3. The Clarifier establishes an in-depth look at the questions posed and possibly puts them together for understanding of their importance in comprehension. Confusing words or sentences along with ideas may need explanation. Doing these tasks calls for a sharing of the story, as do each of the roles.
4. The Summarizer of the story focuses on relating key points of the story, such as in a review of it. Therefore, the exposition with character descriptions and settings respective of time and place would be discussed. This discussion would include things happening in the rising action of the story. Also given attention would be the exciting incidents that lead to decision-making revolving around a climatic moment. And then a coming away from that with the falling action of story. That would be followed by a tying together of events to bring about the close of the story and its overall theme.

HOW TO USE THE RR STRATEGY

With knowing the roles in RR comes the "how" of using this strategy. The main idea is for story comprehension, understanding vocabulary and thoughts, ideas, opinions, and feelings, and at a minimum, knowing the story characters and reactions of those reading the story. Students in a small-group format read aloud a few paragraphs. They may use note taking such as sticky notes and/or underlining if they've their own copy of the story. A teacher or leader pre-read, highlighting to call attention to different portions of the story. And then, of course, the roles already addressed in the previous paragraph taking place when the oral reading is done. Note that the plot of the story is addressed with the use of reach role in this strategy.

Two Points of Interest

This strategy is done mainly in the classroom and in the stated format with roles assigned or chosen. However, a key factor is the "changing" of those titled roles. This is done so that each group member can partake in each responsibility of a role, for best comprehension skill development. The change may happen during a series of reading lessons, as opposed to switching responsibilities at one reading group's meeting. This strategy, while designed for a small group of four, may also be done alone or in a partnership. If done alone, then there should be a taking of notes to review with another person or oneself for personal reflection. If done in a partnership, each member would then take two roles for conversation during the lesson.

Yet, each four-person group may have a student or teacher leader to assist in seeing that the roles are addressed in a formidable manner. Cues may also be offered. In this instance, the leader acts as a guide for the group.

WHO BENEFITS FROM RR AND WHY

For whom and why this reading strategy works best has already been mentioned previously and reiterated here with the main idea that, "Reciprocal Reading is for students who are able to work in cooperative groups." However, the converse of that may be the case with collaboration happening, as group members switch roles and share.

Others for whom this strategy works well include those that need assistance with developmental skills, like being specific, sequencing, evaluating and decision-making, or completing a single task before beginning another one. Practice in the four components helps to differentiate story comprehension through use of the "roles." At the same time, the implementation of these roles impacts students' ability to classify, codify, or systematize the reading passages. Students requiring these types of practices are known as right-hemispheric processors with seeing things holistically. Yet one more benefit of this strategy is for ADHD students. The method has a structure that assists in organization where it's needed. RR may be used as a guide for uncluttering the mind.

This previous processing style may not work for those having left hemispheric dominance. These people are detailed, structured, and spend appropriate time on tasks without taking breaks. They also complete one project at a time while being highly focused, much as an analytic processor would be. Perceptual preferences, such as being auditory, visual, tactile, and kinesthetic, do not influence one's ability to use this strategy effectively. RR reinforces the proclivities of these people and strengthens each of the role's requirements through repetition and exchange of ideas within the group setting. All modalities (auditory, visual, tactual, and kinesthetic) may be in-play with an obvious emphasis on the first two of these.

Oh my, what about dual hemispheric people? Well, these have a combination of the characteristics of the right- and left-brain processors. This hemispheric dominance depends on the situation or may be biologically imposed. Those characteristics involve choosing to work with others or working alone on tasks. Also, they have a propensity sometimes to work on one project such as in their assigned role or a few roles, by sharing responses of each one, simultaneously.

A formal or informal room design is fine, as is sound being present or absent when working on a project. Sometimes there will be taking breaks, which analytic people would not prefer, because they are known to stay on task until they complete work. However, in the RR setting there is an obvious invitation not to take breaks as one is not working alone, and the strategy is structured.

WHY USE RR?

Why do you suppose a teacher or someone reading a book would use the RR strategy? One is to encourage participation skills that have distinct responsibilities. This allows the participator to define their role and at the same time maintain being an active listener. These are people who share and have a discussion style exchange with others in the group.

This reading strategy also involves attention to addressing learning about scaffolding with modeling of how to apply the four roles and guide those using them. Reflective thinking is practiced with each role, as these call for looking at what has been read and/or making predictions based on that. Also, reflection comes with summarizing and, of course, self-actuating, which is the highest metacognitive skill. You may recall that self-actualizing means going forward and taking action. An example would be to observe how a specific educational learning tool is used and then using it.

TYPES OF LITERATURE AND GOALS

The type of literature for this chapter's strategy may be fiction, non-fiction, texts in varied disciplines (science, social studies, and math), and books read that are serious or plausible. It is a method or style of reading not defined by one's age or grade level. An adult could participate in the same manner as easily as those learning to read at an elementary school level. The format of this strategy is like a book talk, which involves examining a story selection in detail for an exchange of ideas and comprehension skill development. But added specificity, from assigned roles. Additionally, the complexity of the book or story selected would vary depending on the ability by age, first language, or perhaps grade level of the readers.

Some advantages of using this RR strategy are that the roles are interchangeable, so the reader experiences different types of comprehension with questions generated by the roles of (a) predictor of events, (b) questioner of what has transpired, and (c) clarifier of the questions posed, statements made, story events, or vocabulary definitions. Each of these roles may bring about more questions, and then the (d) summarizer who relates the sequence and consequences of the story theme closes the reading lesson. This is done by tying together what was read. This is done in a cohesive explanation of the story's theme, characters, and so on.

RR Lesson Plan for Grades 1–4

The following pages provide an example of a lesson plan on the teaching strategy of this chapter. Basically, it is for an elementary school class between grades 1 and 4. However, exceptions can be made for advanced readers. The book selected for this chapter is a rhyming children's picture book and would most likely be for beginning readers. English language learners would benefit from this reading strategy, as there are roles to play that call for application of thinking skills. Also, one should note that, depending on the piece of literature selected, this lesson, especially with the decision-making graphic organizer (DMGO), may be used for those in higher grades.

[The children's book *Sammy Snail's . . . A Little Time for Quiet* has been selected for the RR lesson. This book is applicable for the previously mentioned grades and may be even for pre-school, if it was being read to the students. (Schiering, © 2019)]

The lesson plan begins with a motivation technique to stimulate student learners' interest. What follows is the stating of an objective and activities, questions for each activity, differentiation of instruction, and a choice of three assessments to establish an understanding of the story. The following motivation is done with the entire class, whereas the actual reading lesson will involve several groups of four persons in each group.

MOTIVATION

Picture this: The teacher or leader stands in the classroom with four labels attached by twos with one on each shoulder and one on each wrist. The class can see these labels. Each label is a four-by-six card with a dark-color-printed word on it. These words are the roles in this reading strategy: Predictor, Questioner, Clarifier, and Summarizer.

The teacher asks the class what they suppose these words mean. An example would be, "What does someone who predicts do?" Accepting answers and then dividing the class into small groups of four or five, the teacher distributes, to each group, a paper with the four role titles, and a definition with an example of each one.

Point of Interest: There are, as explained, four roles for RR. However, in some cases there may be a fifth role who would be the teacher or leader who calls on group members to play their role.

Lesson Objective: *The students will be able to identify the four "roles" of this reading strategy and apply them to a book being read in small-group format. To demonstrate comprehension of these roles the students will create an interactive educational game done on a computer or kinesthetically to emphasize the responsibilities of each role, along with story elements involving characters, setting, and events of the story.*

RR Role Cards

1. *Predictor:* Makes a statement about what you think is going to happen in the story. You may use illustrations in the story or the actual text.
   Examples: Based on the book's cover, what do you think is this story's topic? Who do you suppose are some characters? After reading the first page, can you imagine saying or doing what the main character said? Why or why not?
2. *Questioner:* Asks questions to gain an understanding of what's happening in the story. They include literal, applied, and implied comprehension ones.

   Examples: Who was the main character? What was your reaction to this character's personality? What does it mean to glide along a street? Explain your reasoning about the main character's seeking help.

3. *Clarifier:* Makes statements that explain the questions. Examines confusing words, statements, or ideas presented in the story. Assures a shared understanding of the text. Illuminates the story's problem if there is one. *Examples:* The word "glide" means to move with a smooth and continuous motion. The main idea of the story is to have a quiet time each day.
4. *Summarizer:* States the story's main ideas. Goes over events that took place in sequence. Shares ideas about the purpose of the story and its message of it. *Example:* For the book, *Sammy Snail's . . . A Little Time for Quiet*, the main idea is how the snail goes about seeking quiet. This search leads to its going to friends to help solve the problem of noise pollution. The exposition involves the description of the characters and setting. The Rising action relates to the inciting incident. The falling action comes after the story's climatic moment and leads to the solution to the problem with tying all the story elements together. In this story the snail smiles as he experiences a quiet land.

LESSON ACTIVITIES WITH QUESTIONS

1. Each group is given the children's picture book *Sammy Snail's . . . A Little Time for Quiet*. Each group member selects one of the four roles and holds the card to refer to for questions or explanations. This process is respective of their selected roles. The teacher then reads the first page of the book and shows the picture with accompanying questions for each role. Each student goes through their role and asks the following questions that group members are to answer: (*What is your prediction about this story's topic? What is the title of this story? Who is the main character? Where is Sammy? How would you describe this setting? Have you ever glided over a street? Please clarify your answer. How do you move down a street? What do you suppose will happen next? What do you know about the character in the picture? What has happened so far in this story?*)
2. The students, in their groups, continue the reading of the story and conduct their roles as modeled by the teacher. This cooperative reading strategy organizes the roles by addressing the story elements of Characters, Setting, Moods, Events, Problem, and Solution. (*What do you think about the main character? Is it friendly or not? Explain your answer. After Sammy is very sad, what do you think his action will be? Why do you think that? With whom did Sammy speak? How would you

clarify that, and to whom would you speak if you were Sammy? What has happened so far in the story, and where are the places Sammy traveled to? How does Sammy feel about noise? Why? Do you agree or not, and explain your reasoning? What is the story's problem? What role does Buddy Bullfrog play in the story? How does Sammy resolve his problem?)

3. The students in each group, working collaboratively, will create Task Cards for the story elements and RR roles. Then, these will be put on the floor to be put together by the students from different groups. *(What are Task Cards? How can they help you learn about the story's elements of characters, setting, moods, events, problem, and solution? How can these help you comprehend RR's roles? How many Task Cards did your group make? How, if at all, do the other groups' Task Cards differ from your groups? Why do you suppose this is the case? What does the Predictor, Questioner, Clarifier, and Summarizer do with a story? How do the RR roles help you comprehend a story? What are the Predictor's questions in Activity 2?)*

4. The teacher gives the students a set of questions to classify on the front board by category of the four roles in RR. *(What questions go under the Predictor, Questioner, Clarifier, and Summarizer roles? Who can identify questions from each role and how are you able to do that? How many questions are there for each of the RR roles? What question, do you suppose, could be added to each role?)*

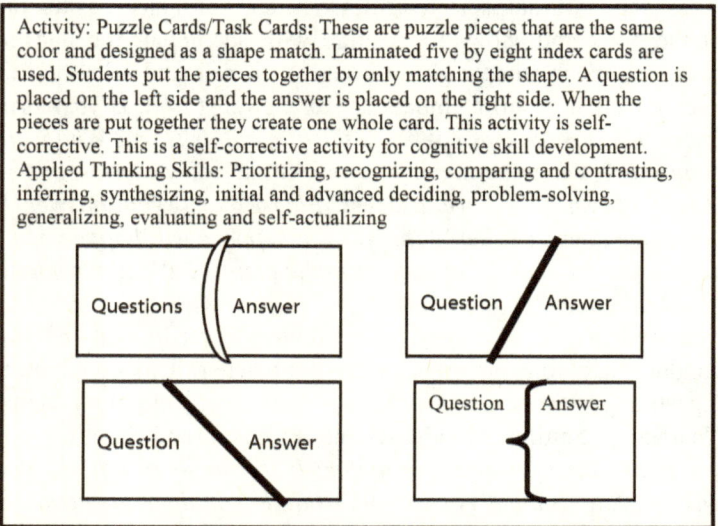

Figure 9.1 Task Cards. *Source:* Schiering, 2001, 2015, 2016.

DIFFERENTIATION OF INSTRUCTION: EXAMPLE: LEARNERS' INTERESTS

The students will separate into selected groups and choose one of the following activities for a class sharing when completed. The group selection will be done by students prioritizing from a list of possible activities that include the following.

1. Creating an illustrated Venn diagram addressing two main characters in the selected piece of literature and showing similarities and differences in actions and/or behavior.
2. Conducting a mock interview of Sammy Snail and Buddy Bullfrog.
3. Configuring slides for a presentation about the story's problem and solution.
4. Making a drawing of each character and setting in the story for a classroom board design.
5. Conducting a scripted role-play of the story conversations in different settings.
6. Designing a Flip-chute and dividing the story's events by type of element (character, settings, moods, events in sequential order, and story problem and solution).
7. Creating a self-corrective educational game for addressing the plot of *Sammy Snail's . . . A Little Time for Quiet* [Schiering, 1974: Master's Thesis on Teacher made educational games and 2013]: A video of six self-corrective educational games, including the Flip Chute, may be found on this author's website: **Creativecognition4U.com**.

Author's Note: Interactive instructional resources, also known as multimodality and experiential or hands-on teaching techniques, are ways to actively engage students in learning a topic. See #7 under the heading, *Differentiation of Instruction: Example: Learners' Interests*. There are three excellent books this author wrote between 2016 and 2019 about these "instructional resources." They're from former students in this author's university class in *Teaching English Language Arts and Reading*. These "activities" may also be referred to as a multimodal, experiential, or a hands-on approach to teaching and learning.

Each activity comes with an illustration in the workbooks, and there are also directions for construction and in-class use. The book titles are *Teaching Creative and Critical Thinking: An Interactive Workbook* (2016), *Achieving Differentiated Learning: Using the Interactive Method Workbook* (2019), and *Special Needs, Different Abilities: The Interactive Method for Teaching and Learning* (2019). The publisher is Rowman and Littlefield, and the author of those books is the same as this one you're reading.

CHARACTER COUNTS AND SOCIAL-EMOTIONAL LEARNING

For this RR lesson, the students create a friendly conversational, cohesive, and comfortable environment with "Affirmation Statements." Examples: *"I like you. You're so kind. You're funny. I love your jacket. Nice hair! You did well on that assignment. I'm proud of you."*

Another Idea: Let's see how you can change a negative statement to a positive one. How to change negative thinking to positive action, such as "Replace the "Don't" statement with the "Do" statement!" = "Don't' stand now for going to the next class!" *"Please remain seated until instructed to go to the next class.* Don't yell. *Please use your inside-the-room voice."*

ASSESSMENT: DMGO

In the book, the main character, Sammy Snail, had to decide about how to stop the noise pollution in the community. At their desks, the students will create a DMGO showing three possible choices that Sammy could use to solve the story problem. One of these is Buddy Bullfrog's suggestion to go both near and far and visit people in their cars, and to talk about working together to stop this situation. If so desired, the DMGO can be done on the computer in small-group format. This way the class is involved in the ever-popular use of technology.

Working in a small-group format, students will select a problem area they think affects them, or those around you and construct a DMGO with the stated problem, three possible solutions, and three possible positive and negative outcomes for each one. The Final Decision and Why this was made complete the organizer. These DMGOs are to be displayed in the classroom with a presentation of the groups' completed DMGO.

CHARACTER COUNTS/SOCIAL-EMOTIONAL LEARNING

In each classroom is an influence of the personalities of the individuals in that space. The combination of these serves as the baseline for a classroom community. You're now asked to think about the classroom atmosphere that best suits learning. This has to be, would you agree, a place that demonstrates those in that space being kind, fair, caring responsible, trustworthy, respectful, and a good citizen? I would think that would be the case at any grade level.

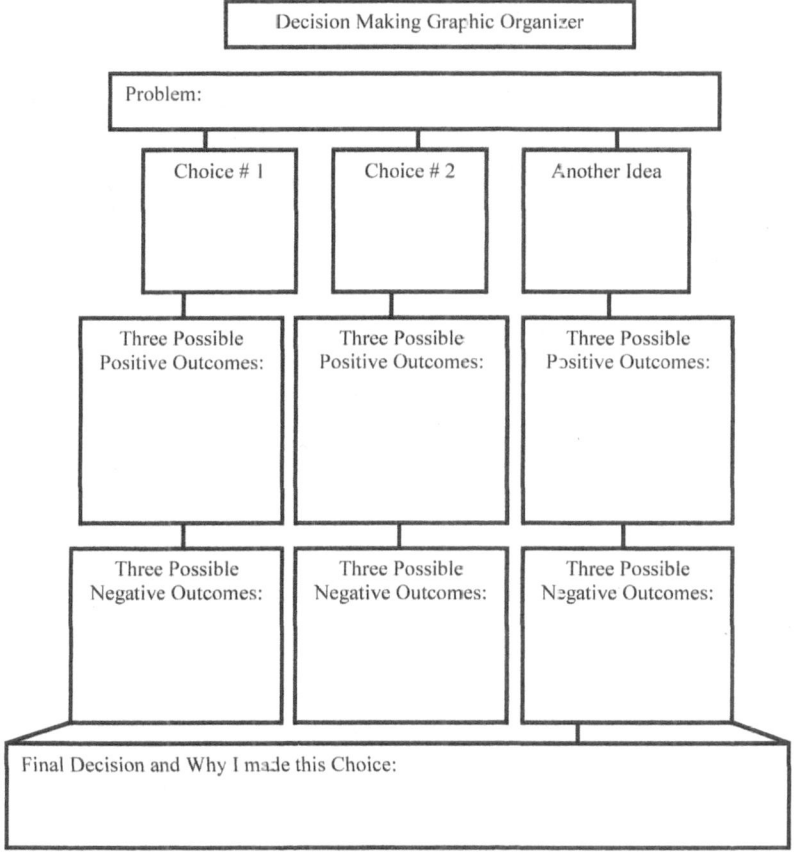

Figure 9.2 DMGO (Decision-Making Graphic Organizer). *Source*: Schiering, 2001, 2015, 2016.

How we teach one to be a person of good character is exhibited in the lessons we plan, types of instruction, questions we ask, and the way they are delivered and answered. One style of presenting is represented not just by what is said, but also how it is said. Facial expressions, body stance, gesturing, and voice tonal quality are all important. All of these should represent being a person of good character for students to emulate.

When the classroom environment is a place of safety, then optimum learning occurs, just because of those factors. For each of the "strategy" chapters in this book the closing portion provides an activity to establish and implement an idea for classroom harmony.

Now that you've seen these examples, form groups of four to six (partnerships work), and have each group make up negative statements and change them to positive ones. Then, each group switches to another group or this exercise may be done as a whole class sharing and post the Don't to Do's on a classroom wall for viewing.

Provide an oral reading of the poem "One Life/Classroom Rule" (Schiering, 1976; 2011), as presented before the close of this chapter. Discuss this poem's last line. In whole class format, glean affirmation statements from the students, and place these on a chart for one week of daily reading silently or aloud. Then, make a copy of these affirmations for students to have on their computers or in their notebooks for reference. Positive thinking and sharing, when done on a regular basis, build one's self-esteem and encourage thoughts about others as well. Positive thinking begets positive thinking.

Continuing Affirmation Statements to other classrooms may be a follow-up done by class members having experienced this Character Counts Activity. Students teaching students is the result with a pleasantry first in the classroom and then in the school. Of course, this is the key point in social-emotional learning, as it brings the class together to form a comfortable and safe atmosphere and shared environment.

Following the poem are some lift-up/affirmation statement examples.

ONE LIFE/CLASSROOM RULE
(Marjorie S. Schiering, 1976; © 2011)

In my early years of classroom teaching
Out of a career spanning quite a few
I came across a situation
That was affecting both the home and school.

No matter where one went,
It brought a loss to everyone's needs
This was "negativity" taking over
In people's thoughts, words, and daily deeds.

So, I reflected for a period of time
About a variety of classroom rules
Like no gum chewing and how to sit
As well as overt and subliminal cues.

The one rule that I wrote and implemented
Was first written in the front of my mind.
I posted it on the classroom wall.
And it worked, well, quite fine.

Honestly, it was undoubtedly very simple
And it impacts individual's feeling good
About their personal self-worth and value.
If all used it, it surely would

Create a community of caring.
One that promotes with incessant reason
A sense that there is thoughtfulness
In our sharing, regardless of the season.

It's a rule for daily living
Without bias being displayed
With positive self-esteem the result
And it demonstrates a good "give-away."

Here's the rule for living
The best way that one can:
To care about what one is saying.
Without sarcasm, we'll really be trans-

formative in what we're doing
With getting/ giving a very big plus
The rule to which I refer is:

"NO Put Downs ... *Only Lift UPS!*

EXAMPLE: AFFIRMATION STATEMENTS

I like you. We are amazing. You are beautiful. Kindness will always come back. Let go of negative energy. We are all strong Never give up. You can make a difference. Love yourself. Always move forward. When you are down, you can come back up. We work well together. Kindness will always come back to you. Move forward. We can make a difference. Thank you.

Now it's your turn to make a list of affirmative statements you may say to yourself and others. Let's start with: "You're a good friend. You did well with your 'role' using Reciprocal Reading. I'm proud of you because...."

Questions:

1. *What types of differentiation of instruction did you evidence being done in this chapter?*
2. *What was your favorite activity and why did you select that one?*
3. *Why is Reciprocal Reading attributed to those who like structure?*

Chapter 10

Orton–Gillingham Strategy

Catherine Colonna

THE STRATEGY

History

Orton–Gillingham was among the first teaching approaches designed to help struggling readers by explicitly teaching the connections between letters and sounds. In the 1930s, neuropsychiatrist and pathologist Dr. Samuel T. Orton and educator/psychologist Anna Gillingham developed the Orton–Gillingham approach to reading instruction for students with "word blindness," which would later become known as dyslexia. Their approach combined direct, multi-sensory teaching strategies paired with systematic, sequential lessons focused on phonics (https://www.understood.org › articles › Orton Gillingham-...).

STRATEGY EXPLANATION

The Orton–Gillingham strategy is a multisensory approach to teaching decoding and spelling. By using the senses of sight, hearing, and touch, students are able to divide a word into syllables in order to read the word and spell it. Once students have mastered this technique, they are able to recognize words more quickly than they had previously. This word recognition allows for putting sentences together and later comprehending what has been related because they can now easily read. Or, in other words; as the students become fluent in their decoding, their understanding of what they have read improves.

MORE THAN TEACHING SOUNDS

While many think that this strategy is about teaching sounds, it is actually more than that. The three Orton–Gillingham strategies this author has found invaluable for teaching decoding and spelling are as follows:

A. Syllable Types

1. *Syllable Type*: Closed Syllable. *Description:* This is represented in the examples with a consonant and a short vowel followed by a consonant. A closed syllable, therefore, is one vowel "closed in" by a consonant and a "syllable" is a word or word part with one talking vowel. Syllables are also explained as being a unit of pronunciation having one vowel sound. *Examples:* C*a*n, p*e*g, d*i*m, r*o*t, t*u*b.
2. *Syllable Type:* Vowel Consonant – e: *Description:* This occurs when a vowel is made long by adding "e" to the end of the word or syllable. *Examples:* C*a*ne, th*e*me, d*i*me, r*o*te, and t*u*be.
3. *Syllable Type:* Open Syllable: *Description:* A long vowel at the start of a word or syllable. *Examples:* *A*corn, *e*vent, *i*sland, *o*mit, and h*u*mid.
4. *Syllable Type:* Diphthong: *Description:* Two vowels together that make one sound. The first vowel carries the sound. *Examples:* M*ai*l, p*ai*nt gl*ow*, emp*ow*er, p*ea*l, empl*oy*, s*ou*l, s*ou*nd, f*ou*nd, kn*ea*d, pl*ay*, and s*oi*l.
5. *Syllable Type*: R-controlled syllable: *Description:* A vowel followed by the letter "r" changes the vowel sound. *Examples:* F*ar*, nev*er*, sw*ir*l, st*or*m, and ch*ur*n.
6. *Syllable Type*: Consonant-le: *Description:* "le," when coming at the end of a word has the "e" as silent. *Examples*: ab*le*, scrib*ble*, wob*ble*, peb*ble*, and jug*gle*.

B. Dividing Syllables

Teaching how to divide a word into syllables (this list of syllable divisions is adapted from the *Gillingham Manual*, Anna Gillingham and Bessie W. Stillman. Cambridge and Toronto: Educators Publishing Service, 1997).

1. Identify the vowels in the word, b*u*tt*o*n.
2. Identify the consonants that separate the vowels in the word bu*tt*on.
3. Divide the word button into syllables. Then, write these syllables. But/ton.
4. Say the syllables. (Same as above done in auditory fashion.)
5. Does this sound familiar? Why or why not?
6. Is there another way to divide the word? If so, what is it?

7. If there is, then start again.

C. Teaching Finger Spelling

1. Say the word. (Auditory)
2. Repeat the word. (Auditory)
3. Segment the sounds of the word. As one segments the word, one taps or holds up a finger for each sound. (Auditory/kinesthetic)
4. Then, as each sound is repeated, write the corresponding letters. (Visual/auditory/kinesthetic)

FOR WHOM THIS STRATEGY IS BENEFICIAL

The Orton–Gillingham approach assists students who have difficulty reading or comprehending words, interpreting letters and other symbols. These learning difficulties do not affect their overall intelligence. This strategy is helpful because students use more than one of their senses to learn new sounds. When I teach my students a new sound, I tell them, "The more senses you use, the better you will remember the sound and then the word." For example, when I recite the "sh" sound, I ask my students to repeat the sound three times while tracing the letters on their desks with their fingers. Here the students are using multiple perceptual preferences or the auditory, visual, and tactile processing senses.

Over my twenty-year career, I also have found this strategy assistive for children who come from multicultural backgrounds where English has not been their first language. Additionally, students who may be performing below grade level in reading have benefitted from Orton–Gillingham instructional techniques. Furthermore, this strategy is good for individual use, as it's structured and follows a sequence in an analytic fashion. Partnerships may be used and benefit those who need the support of classmates and camaraderie.

WHY THIS STRATEGY IS BENEFICIAL

This strategy provides a set of rules and guidelines for students to follow. Such structure is helpful to analytic processors who like to work alone and need individual attention when involved with reading and spelling. Additionally, those who like to see the whole picture see the whole word, and this approach is most appealing because these students like to see the end result, as opposed to sequencing as the only means for presentation of the material.

Another reason why this strategy is useful is that it provides patterns and structure which are enjoyed by those who require organization and learn best when things are done in this fashion. Most importantly, this strategy provides a multi-modality approach with work done in auditory, visual, tactile, and kinesthetic perceptual preferences. The learner benefits from having all of these addressed to meet their needs in reading.

The idea of structure is appreciated by analytic processors who like working on one project at a time to completion, as opposed to many projects not necessarily to completion. The strategy allows for scope and sequence and, most importantly, as stated earlier, this is a multi-modality approach to decoding. All perceptual preferences of the learner are in play at any given time for instruction.

ORTON–GILLINGHAM LESSON PLAN

Background Information

This lesson was created for my class of first-grade students from multicultural backgrounds. Students with Individualized Education Plans (IEPs) were also included. The strategy can easily be used in small groups or for individual instruction. This particular plan was designed to help my class with comprehension of closed syllables. It builds upon students' prior knowledge of sounds, which in this case included most short vowels, consonants, and consonant blends.

LEARNING OBJECTIVE 1 AND CLASSROOM SETTING

Students will be able to identify and create closed syllables by recognizing short vowel sounds and later writing sentences with these words. Then, they will read closed syllable words from Flash Cards and identify the short vowel in each word. Next, they will spell words with sounds previously taught but were misread in those lessons (*More than Teaching Sounds A-1*).

The classroom setting has students seated in pairs at their desks and facing the classroom Smart Board.

LEARNING OBJECTIVE 2

The second half of this lesson introduces new material, by making a connection to prior knowledge. The students will be able to recognize short vowels a, e, i, o, and u, as a result of having met the first lesson objectives through the presented activities. Additionally, by knowing that a closed syllable is one vowel closed in by a consonant and a syllable is a word or word part with one talking vowel, the students will be able to realize and recognize a list of closed syllable words.

MOTIVATION

The teacher will have taped to their arms examples on index cards of closed syllable words. These may include, but are not limited to, the following: dim, lamp, sit, sat, pet, mop, top, chug, and much.

ACTIVITIES FOR OBJECTIVE #1 WITH QUESTIONS

1. The students will review the prior sounds taught. *(What is the closed vowel in the word "can?" How would you describe your knowing the location of this vowel? What is the closed vowel in the word "peg"? Where is this short vowel located, and what are the letters that surround it on either side? What is the closed vowel in the word "dim," and what letters close it? What is the closed vowel for the word "rot"? What other letters surround this vowel, and where are they located?)*
2. Students read a series of projected Flash Cards that display different sounds presented in previous lessons. Examples include: ay, ch: chill chip, chat, such, chop, chugs, chips, chum, chops, and much. (Please note that this is an example list. However, teachers need to use their judgment in selecting words in accordance with student performance, i.e., words misread in previous lessons.) Each word appears on a Flash Card and is read with the following questions. *(What is the closed short vowel sounds in the following words? in chill, chip, chat, such, shop, chugs, chips, chum, chops, much? What are the letters that close in these short vowels?)*
3. Students spell words with sounds previously presented but misspelled. (A sample set follows with questions.) Using your hearing skills and then your voice, when called upon, read the following words that I am saying. I will write the word on the Smart Board as you spell it. Answer the following questions when asked to share. *(How do you spell cat, home, sob, hot, rub, stun, gate, cabs, crop, and rig? What is the short vowel sounds in each word? What are the letters that surround the short vowel? How do you suppose you knew how to spell the words? What is*

82   Chapter 10

your personal reaction to the application of this word-spell work? Why do you think or feel that?)
4. Students write dictated sentences that contain closed short vowel sounds. (Write the sentence, "The dog ran home for a bone." What is the closed short vowel sound in each word? How were you able to identify it? What is the closed short vowel sound in each word of this sentence? The chilly dog sat. How were you able to write and recognize this sound? What do you think is the next thing we'll do with learning about decoding, spelling, and sounds of words?)

ACTIVITIES FOR OBJECTIVE #2

1. *Making a connection* to prior knowledge from the first objective, the students will recognize the short vowel sounds of a, e, i, o, and u. *(What are the short vowel sounds? What are some short vowel sounds?)*
2. *Realizing a closed syllable* is one vowel closed in by a consonant, and a syllable is a word or word part with one being the talking vowel, the students will read (auditory activity) a list of closed syllable words and give an example or explanation of the word (comprehension activity). Examples of closed syllable words: ham, sun, tab, fun, hen, pin, top, vet. *(What are the eight words presented? Say each one correctly using good pronunciation. What is the meaning of each word? Describe or give an example of the word. The first one, "ham," is a food item.)*
3. *Visual and auditory activity:* The students will be shown a poster drawing of the words met, not, hen, and wed. The last letter of each word will have a drawing of a see-through door covering it. The students are to identify the letter that is a "door closing" on a closed syllable *(What consonant closes the short vowel [closed syllable] "met"? What is the short vowel in this word? What is the consonant that closes the door on the short vowel [closed syllable] in the word "not?" What is the closed syllable in this word? What are the consonants "close the door" on the words "hen" and "wed"? What is the closed syllable/short vowel in those words?)*
4. *Phonemic awareness activity:* The students will decide if the sound presented is a closed syllable or not. In a game-style approach, the students will collaborate with a partner as the teacher reads closed and not closed syllable words with short vowel sounds. Each partnership will use its whiteboard to record the word "yes" or "no," depending on the word given. This may also be done on a shared sheet of numbered paper.

   Students hold up their answers with positive teacher reinforcement. The possible list of words: rab, is, dex, tw, bit, and me. *(What is a closed* syllable word? How do you know if you hear a closed syllable word with the vowel being short? What type of word is rob? How do you know this? Is "me" a closed syllable word? How do you know this? How did you like using your whiteboards and/or making the list of "yes" or "no" answers?)

DIFFERENTIATION OF INSTRUCTION ACTIVITIES

1. Oral Reading: The student will read a list of words with closed syllables. Sample List: tin, flag, hum, den, mob, and jet. (*What are the short vowels in each word? How do you know this? What are some closed syllable words you know?* Share these with your classmates.)
2. Spelling Words: The students will write a list of closed syllable words using finger spelling. Sample list: jam, red, blog, six, run, and fox. (What is the closed syllable in each word? How do know how to spell each word?)
3. Read Sentences: Students will read sentences with closed syllable words. Sample sentences include: "The fox has a dim den." "Jack got a box of red pins."

SUGGESTIONS FOR EXTENDING THE LESSON

1. Students may work in pairs to go on a word hunt in books available for reading in our classroom.
2. Students can identify closed syllable words they hear in a song like, "Old MacDonald."

ASSESSMENT

Students will be given magnetic letters. These are to be placed on a teacher-provided magnet board to show closed syllable words. At least five words per student with one representative of each short vowel sound.

Character Counts and Social-Emotional Learning (SEL) *The "Activity" section for Objectives 1 and 2 addresses character and SEL, through the collaboration and cooperation of students' discussing and being involved in these activities. That includes the accompanying questions upon which each small group or partnership participated in talking with one another, either during the lesson or at another time.*

Having students actively involved in suggestions one and two for extending the lesson provides another opportunity for communication with one another where SEL comes naturally. Often, collaborating finds individuals going beyond the topic at hand as they explore their abilities and share generally about the lesson.

Yet another idea regarding character counts and SEL is to have students design and create an in-class bulletin board providing an outdoor scene with a pathway with examples of closed syllable words. Some of these may form a sentence. Subsequently, as students walk the path, they say the word, and relate the closed short vowel sound, in a different color than the color of the other letters. In some cases, these words may form a sentence. Example of a sentence with closed syllable words with one-after-another: "T*i*m s*a*t *i*n the s*u*n *o*n a m*a*t." Students may make a small illustration to show the action of a sentence when applicable.

ONE MORE THOUGHT: A REITERATION

The Orton–Gillingham reading strategy calls for ongoing teacher involvement in setting the parameters of a lesson. It is important to demonstrate continual reinforcement by praising students for their accomplishments. While repetition is often necessary when using this strategy, bringing forth positivity is noted through teacher participation and modeling of how students are to reinforce positive attitudes with classmates. Demonstrating how to make positive statements when classmates share is important for classroom cohesiveness and comfort.

Chapter 11

Reader's and Writer's Workshop

Natalie Simpson-White and Daniel Berger

R&WW: STRATEGY EXPLANATION

To begin, you are asked to note the word "and" that is between Reader's and Writer's Workshop (R&WW). This conjunction, "and," is there because this is a dual strategy. Additionally, guess what, the strategy is intermingled in that reading enables writing and what one writes is based on what one reads. This strategy is teacher-led. And that leading activity is to ensure students' active involvement in the workshop.

Regarding the reading portion of this strategy, the teacher selects an area of reading that is to be addressed. This selection may involve: (1) grammar and punctuation, as much as (2) identifying the elements of a story, or (3) decoding words, (4) fluency in reading, (5) accuracy in reading, which includes, (6) vocabulary, (7) comprehension with identity of prior knowledge, (8) making predictions as is evidenced in Reciprocal Reading. (9) recognizing applied and inferential sentences and paragraphs, (10) relating the six elements of a story in short answer format, as well as (11) personalizing the story to one's own reactions, thoughts, and feelings.

The students practice the selected topic during independent reading and writing time. This strategy empowers students to rely on themselves and develop a sense of self-efficacy, with respect to the formation of students' reading and writing abilities and, afterward, the application of these in everyday situations. Perhaps the most interesting is that different groups may work on different skills applied to individual work as well. The teacher serves as an introducer and guide for which a reading selection may best be suited for a designated lesson.

Discovery of one's own skills comes into play, as students are given latitude with respect to meeting and honing their reading and writing applications, respective of (a) varied genres of books and (b) types of writing. These are addressed whether formal, informal, creative, informational, persuasive, author's intent/purpose, understanding/comprehension, author's messages, thinking skills and storytelling formats, to name a few.

Reader's Workshop

This strategy does not have a starting age or age limit. Subsequently, it may be used at any grade level from kindergarten through the high school years or beyond. One of the main purposes for this type of workshop is to create confident readers who show purpose and determination with what? Reading and Writing! Also, indications are that students, with continued use of reading, will develop an appreciation for written material, especially with respect to interest areas.

The overall idea regarding the R&WW is that over time, highly varied literature topics are available, and students read what they like. Such selection may run the gambit from (a) fantasy fiction, (b) sports, (c) hobbies, (d) mysteries, (e) varied forms of poetry, (f) true stories involving real life events, (g) historical fiction, (h) novels about issues facing a particular town or the whole world, and (i) science fiction. How an individual develops a particular taste for literature depends in part to what the student has been exposed in formative years and beyond.

Students work on skill development when reading and then writing. Additionally, students may be in Guided Reading groups where they are separated by *ability levels*. In this case, a common text topic is used, introduced to the group by emphasizing the topic of the lesson. The teacher listens and watches the students' reading. The group or teacher may ask questions.

R&WW: Choice of Literature

Preferred books depend on separating students by interest areas. Subsequently, one or several students may prefer books about: sports, fiction, gaming, computer-generated literature with serious stories or humorous ones, or even newspaper literature. Student "choice" of literature is a key factor in the reading portion of R&WW. In the starting months of using this strategy, the students may be given "teacher-selected" literature to read. This approach is mainly for students having the opportunity to experience varied story topics and formats. However, the "choice" part would come with the students divided into two to five groups, depending on class size. And then would be the students electing their own book or story to read.

Next, they choose from stories the teacher provides. This application is the beginning of student empowerment. Additionally, working in small group formats by student choice may build friendships, as this strategy allows for working with a partner. Of course, reading alone is also available. Regardless of the book or story selected for reading the students become "independent" thinkers as they analyze and reflect on reading material for analysis and evaluation.

How to Use the Reading Workshop

There are four components of Reader's Workshop. These include:

1. A Mini Lesson: The teacher introduces a topic for the lesson. A read-aloud of a short story, such as those in this book's chapter 16, focuses on messages in the story, vocabulary comprehension, plot, and teacher modeling of reading style. The purpose of this portion of the R&WW includes introduction of a common topic, noting reading style or oral presentation techniques, examining the selected story, and addressing story elements. Also, of import is allowing some student choice regarding the topic of a story. Character analysis may occur, as well as story sequence and one's personal reaction to the story.
2. Independent Reading: This is a time of thirty to forty-five minutes when the students have uninterrupted time to read alone.
3. Conferring/Conferencing: The teacher discusses the format (book, story, poem, and so on) chosen for Independent Reading. These focus on comprehension or topics chosen by the teacher and addressed in the Lesson Plan that follows this section of the chapter. This time is for teacher–student engagement with conferencing on what has been done in this forty-five to sixty-minute period. The teacher provides questions for students to answer in oral and/or journaling formats, which involve the Writer's Workshop. A set of questions may be provided for students to answer in oral and/or journaling formats, which involve the Writer's Workshop.
4. Sharing Time: This allows whole-class involvement and students' reflection on their reading. Areas of importance include what they learned, and/or areas of ease, difficulties, or indifference, if experienced. Sharing is vital, as it provides for students' owning their reactions to Independent Reading and certainly addresses SEL as students interact conversationally.

Writer's Workshop Strategy

Overall, the idea of the Writer's Workshop is to provide a time for writing when the students are engaged in only that activity. They may use different genres, or a teacher-selected one. In the case of the latter the students may do Guided Writing with one group working with the scope and sequence of writing and another writing in a specific genre. The idea is to match the student to the writing type where the student benefits from practicing writing.

This workshop is student-centered with the concepts that students learn to write best when writing frequently for extended periods of time and on topics of their choosing. This time period allows students to develop their skills with teacher guidance if needed. One further point is that when students are working in small-group format, the teacher may select a topic to write about or suggest a topic.

How to Use the Writer's Workshop

Mini Lessons: These usually run for about ten to twenty minutes and are used for teacher-guided examples of different genres of writing. You'll want, first, to instruct on the progression and organization of writing, which include the following:

a. Pre-writing: This is when the writer (author) thinks about the topic to be addressed and may discuss it with others. The use of a graphic organizer might come in handy to arrange ideas in a desired order. Gathering research on a topic is part of this process.
b. Revising: Have a quiet reading of what has been written. Mark places with a pencil where you desire to make changes. Remain on the topic. Use adjectives and collaborate with a classmate or partner to see if changes might be made.
c. Drafting: This is the placing of your thoughts, ideas, opinions, judgments, and feelings onto paper in sentence and paragraph form about the topic you have chosen. The important part of this step is the organization of your writing.
d. Editing: Check sentences for punctuation, each one beginning with a capital letter, check spelling and grammar. Have a partner assist with editing if you're not writing alone.
e. Publishing: Construct your final draft with illustrations if part of your story needs that. Share your completed story with others, and
f. Evaluating: Reread your writing and revise if necessary. Decide if this is your best writing.

Writing from different perspectives or points of view (first or third person), elements of a story, and character descriptions are a few of the places you'd use the (a) through (f) steps that were just explained for what to do when writing. Some writing steps follow:

1. Independent Writing: This is an extended period devoted to writing what was presented in the Mini Lesson. The area of concentration includes the organization of a written piece with students forming a narrative in a specified genre.

There may be journal writing on a specified topic, and using varied language or style of writing, such as rhyming poetry.

2. Conferring/Mid-workshop Teaching: This procedure has the teacher visiting the groups to see what each is doing. Providing suggestions and asking students how things are going, and then keeping a record of student progress are part of this conferring process (fifteen to thirty minutes)
3. Sharing: This is a time for students to confer with one another by sharing their writing. It's a time to discuss and present not just the writing, but also classmates' reactions to it.

WHO BENEFITS FROM R&WW AND WHY

One of the major benefits of this dual strategy is for students to have structure and organization with respect to the four steps beginning with a Mini-Lesson in Reader's Workshop. This workshop provides direction for the upcoming independent work times, working with a partner or in small groups (McDavid, 2004). Subsequently, students have extended time to hone their reading and writing skills. They may possibly develop a sincere liking of literature, and certainly discerning genres, author's intent, awareness of prior knowledge, and acquisition from newly read material of their choosing. Students are exposed to a variety of book topics, types, and styles. They may work by themselves or in partnerships or groups, allowing for self-reflection or collaboration with peers.

To students' benefit, this dual strategy allows for small-group and whole-class discussion. The sharing time and those who need specified time-periods with SEL may enjoy the camaraderie allotted for with R&WW. How? This is accomplished, as communication with one another is a culminating activity. Sharing is built into the program to provide exposure to opinions of others while encouraging acceptance of one's work. Interestingly, those who like to see the whole picture or end-product can know that by experiencing the writing and sharing at the close of the workshops. And those who favor the scope and organized flow of a lesson have the outlined sequence. Also, when Writer's Workshop is used, obviously, the students become the authors of their own work. This strategy has something for everyone.

Students have time to read and write on their own and digest information while having the teacher's guidance. Another benefit of this strategy is allowing leveled groups to meet, knowing they may address comfortably, a particular skill according to the student's needs. It's easily observable that grouping provides for differentiation of instruction, whether through interest groups, time on task, ability level, pace, and kinds of instruction (behaviorist, experientialist, passive recipients, learner's needs, styles, or tier lessons).

With respect to processing styles, learners may address their own preferences. They may have an ending "product" that relates to their perceptual preferences (auditory, visual, tactile, or kinesthetic), or several of these. Students learn to think for themselves frequently as writers.

When you read the heading of this section, did you think the grade level span was huge? Certainly, it is just that. So, you might wonder why that is. Well, it's because the pieces that have been selected for reading will be interpreted based on one's prior knowledge about the topic. Therefore, the higher the grade level, the more advanced the application of cognitive skills will likely be. And delving into analysis of the story, along with not just overt, but subliminal messages tend to be deepest based on the level of one's experiences. Regardless, the use of recalling and reflection along with evaluation and analysis are important cognitive components for this R&WW.

Strategies within this singular strategy form the "why" one would use R&WW. This selection includes making connections to past experiences and bringing them to the present with comparison and contrast. Also included is visualizing the material presented or written about by making pictures in one's head about how the reading assists in comprehension of the reading material.

Drawing conclusions from one's reading and writing is evident with inferences made by reading between the lines. In this case, context clues, picture clues, and finding meaning are practiced. This strategy helps readers determine the purpose of the reading material and ascertain, through self-analysis, and group discussions how it may impact their lives or the lives of others. Then, synthesizing the reading selection benefits students in consolidating presented information.

When it comes to the Writer's Workshop, there are six things that should be known and (Great source iWrite, 2006) these include establishing ideas for writing with (1) purpose, (2) focus, (3) organizing writing with a beginning, middle, and end, (4) practicing with story elements and voice, which is done in accordance with first, second, or third person accounting. Then there is (5) word choice, with attention to parts of speech used in the writing. Another advantage or "why" of this strategy is (6) varying sentences in length with a smooth flow to the passage editing for grammar, punctuation, capitalization, and spelling.

Sharing is a natural byproduct of Writer's Workshop. However, students should not be forced to share, as some may feel uncomfortable and it's important to note that the major factor in any of the Reading Strategies is to allow for students' feeling at ease and calm in their classroom environment.

LESSON PLAN IDEAS

One story from chapter 16 of this book has been used for teacher or student choice of topic, as well as with the four components of the Reader's Workshop. Commencing with the Reader's Mini Lesson there is an intertwining and following through with Writer's Workshop. The entire process should take several weeks, but at a minimum two weeks.

LESSON PLAN FOR R&WW FOR GRADES 2–12+ (SCHIERING, 2023). THIS LESSON PLAN IS BASED ON THE RESEARCH OF THIS CHAPTER'S AUTHORS NATALIE SIMPSON-WHITE AND DANIEL BERGER.

MOTIVATION

The teacher will use the internet to show the video *Five Ways to Stop Bullying*. This may be found at https://youtu.be/vGV5jzPYvmo. Further information will be presented from the article Eradicating Bullying (Schiering, J. 2014-2021: See Addendum in this chapter).

LESSON OBJECTIVES FOR A TEACHER-SELECTED STORY

For the introduction of this strategy, the author selected the "Digging for a Fossil: A Bullying Story" from chapter 16 of this book. Whereas student choice of a story or book would be the norm, for the purpose of this lesson plan, one story has been selected to represent the R&WW strategy.

OBJECTIVES

1. The students' gaining knowledge of what this case of bullying entails and how it was stopped. They identify the roles of bully, victim, and protector.
2. The students' evidence, through reading a first-person account of the teacher's being bullied as a child, and how these roles played out in her life.

3. The students use the thinking skills of analyzing and evaluating, comparing and contrasting responses to the bullying story with journaling using a teacher-created questionnaire.

ACTIVITIES FOR OBJECTIVES 1–5 USING THE R&WW STRATEGY (SEE FIGURE 11.1)

1. The students, after being introduced to the story, through a teacher reading the first page, will read the story aloud in their small groups.
2. The students will follow the R&WW steps, and then, working as a group, they will fill in a Story Map Graphic Organizer about the story. These organizer elements are Characters, Setting, Moods, Events (at least five in sequence), Problem, and Solution.
3. The students will post their story maps on the class smart board and compare, and contrast these for accuracy, analysis, sequencing, and comprehension of how the other groups envisioned the six story elements.
4. The students will select their own story topic, which may match the one read, in class, or another selection from this book's chapter 16, or a topic that addresses an interest area.
5. Students will create their own Story Map graphic organizer on their selected topic. Then, over a week or two, they will write their story using the story elements and present this story to the class, orally. Guidelines for an Oral Presentation will serve as the assessment tool. See part II, chapter 7, for a listing of these guidelines.

INTEGRATION OF THE R&WW: STEPS

Mini Lesson and Independent Reading: These have already been described with the students' having a teacher reading of page one *Digging for a Fossil*. Following this the students will work in groups and, taking turns, read the story aloud to group mates. This reading is to be done with voice modulation and facial expressions to match the moods of the story. Gesturing and body stance are to be done in accordance with the events of the story.

Conferencing/ Conferring, and Writer's Workshop: These portions of R&WW take place over a few days, possibly a week. The students will be given a teacher-created list of journal questions that address the story's content, and their personal reactions to the story. The students write their answers. Then, the teacher, visiting each group, will discuss the story's content. The students interact with the teacher in relating their answers to the questions.

At the very least this is a time when the students come to know personal reactions of their group regarding bullying. Additionally, the teacher will read the students' responses to the questions, encourage their participation, and offer inspiration regarding the answers to questions discussed in the group setting. This portion of the lesson involves independent journal writing and conferring from the section on *"How to Use the Writer's Workshop."*

Journaling and Discussion Questions

1. Who were the characters in the story, and where and when did it take place?
2. What was the topic of the story and what does it mean to bully someone? (Have you experienced being bullied? If so, explain your answer by relating the incident in your Journal.)
3. What was the connection between fossil hunting and bullying, and what were the three main events of the story? You may identify more if so desired.
4. What were the problems and solutions of the story?
5. What role do you play or think you would play when bullying happens?
6. Are you the victim with a voice or not? Why or why not?
7. Are you like the protector in the story? Explain your answer.
8. Who might a "protector" be in a classroom, if not you, and why do you think that?
9. What is your reaction to this story and why is that?
10. Who are your friends, and how would you help them if any needed assistance?
11. What are words that show concern or respect for someone? [Select one and write a time when you were that or saw that.]
12. If you have never been bullied, what do you suppose your reaction would be if you were "Sal?"
13. What might you have done in this situation to help "Sal?" Why?
14. What is your overall reaction to this story? Explain your answer.
15. Think of a time when you helped someone. Please share that experience in your small group.

Sharing Time: This portion of R&WW involves social-emotional learning (SEL), as students share their answers to the journal questions with the teacher and/or group mates.

EXTENDING THE LESSON REGARDING READING AND WRITING

1. The students will be introduced to the elements on a Story Map graphic organizer. This form, as seen in the following illustration, is to be filled-in by the groups collaborating on what goes in each section.
2. Following the creation of the Story Map, the students will place their groups' work on the classroom smart board for a comparison of story

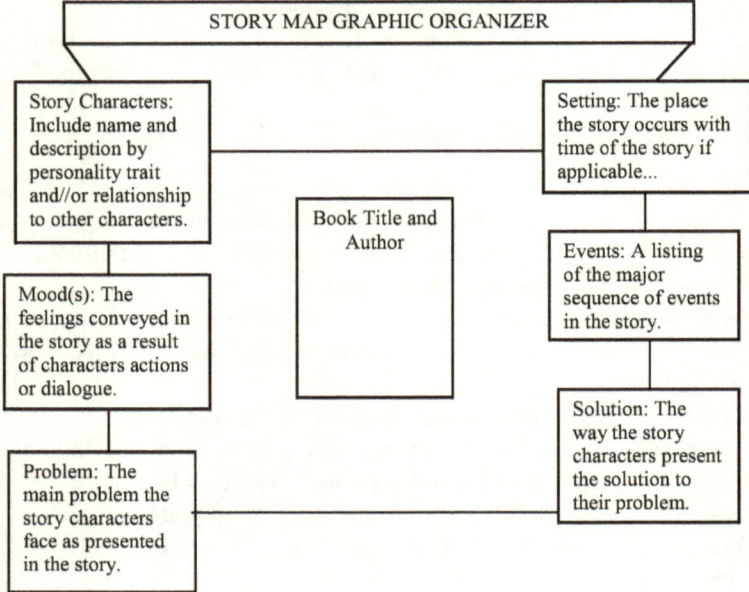

Figure 11.1 **Story Map Graphic Organizer.** *Source*: Schiering, 2015.

elements. These are to be viewed, discussed, compared, contrasted, analyzed, and evaluated for comprehension of the story. Students are to take notes on their reactions to each group's Story Map.

DIFFERENTIATION OF INSTRUCTION IDEA

1. The students, individually, will select a topic of their choosing and create a Story Map with all six elements addressed. They must use the format of the graphic organizer as seen in the Illustration ____ for their story.
2. The students will, individually, using the story elements, write a story for classroom sharing. This story may be on the topic of this lesson, or one that would address an interest area of students in the class.
3. The students will present their story to the class.
4. The students may choose to write creatively (imaginative) or informatively (fact-based) while they are self-actuating with the creation of the story.
5. The students will write a new ending to the story and read it during R&WW.

ASSESSMENT

Using the *Guidelines for an Oral Presentation* in part II, chapter 7, the students will respond to each criterion, in narrative format, and give these to the teacher and the individual presenting the story. Furthermore, the teacher, using these evaluations, will record the students' responses on a Tally Sheet for individual student reference and emphasis on positive statements.

CHARACTER COUNTS AND SEL

The video used as motivation for this lesson plan began a discussion about bullying. Identity of the roles of bully, victim, and protector were also examined and discussed. At this juncture the class will be provided with the modified *Eradicating Bullying* article by Joshua Schiering, 2021 (see Addendum in this chapter). The review of the article will encourage students to share their personal reactions to this article's suggestions for stopping bullying and realizing the victim has a voice. Additionally, the class will discuss and ascertain what the term "follow through" means when someone has been bullied.

Using the QR Code on p. 96, the students will evidence the role of "Protector," as explained by Thomas Edison. In the video he refers to his mother as this type of person. She became his teacher when he wasn't doing well in school. She homeschooled her son. A discussion with classmates reviews the questions previously journaled with an emphasis on what each of us may do to thwart bullying. This refers to different forms of bullying such as physical and/or verbal abuse, harassment, discrimination, and prejudice. The main idea is to have the class form a unified image of anti-bullying strategies. If time allows, the students may create a video addressing the effects of bullying and ways to prevent it for other classes to view.

ADDENDUM

ERADICATING BULLYING
BY JOSHUA SCHIERING

From the article's author: "When you apply the tenants of the following article you will create a social-emotionally safe environment. This is for your students and fellow faculty. Positiveness combined with zero tolerance for meanness will serve as an empowering example. I encourage all of us to lead by example!" (Schiering, J., 2023)

Two negative make a positive, right? . . . Not when it comes to bullying!

Figure 11.2 QR Code. *Source*: Schiering, 2016.

A single negative comment or act can have a lifelong and irreversible impact on a person. Whether in camps, schools, families, playgrounds, and even playgroups, bullying is a natural part of our culture. But, it doesn't have to be that way anymore. As individuals, we are empowered to make decisions about our actions. How we react to what we see and hear is up to each person. When it comes to bullying, I always challenge my staff and children to be counter-cultural in their decision making,

Bullying (Verb: ˈbo͝olē) (http://wikipedia.org.wiki/abuse)

Use of superior strength, influence, force, threat, or coercion designed to abuse, intimidate, or to aggressively impose domination over others. The behavior is often repeated and habitual while there is an imbalance of social or physical power. Bullying may consist of one or more of these four basic types of abuse: emotional, verbal, physical, and cyber.

Synonyms: persecute, oppress, tyrannize, browbeat, harass, torment, intimidate, strong-arm, dominate.

Is It Bullying?

Some say the term "bullying" is overused and doesn't apply to all cases of meanness.

I say, "Listen to the victim!" So, who gets to decide if an action is "bullying?" The answer is clear and simple, "The victim alone decides if they are being bullied." While a single act of calling someone a name may not appear to fit into the definition of bullying, I challenge us all to take a closer look. Did being called that name makes the victim feel intimidated? Did the name caller have an implied power differential over the victim? As a result of this action, did the victim have a hard time focusing on schoolwork? Were they afraid of a repeat of the action? Did they feel oppressed? When it comes to feelings, well, no one gets to tell someone else what they are feeling. Therefore, the victim decides if he/she is being bullied. Period! End of discussion.

Take It Seriously!

As educators and role models we must take every reported and observed act of meanness seriously. While as adults we may have thicker skin and our life experiences help us handle the intimidating actions of a bully, the issue a child is facing might be the most significant and "biggest deal" in their lives. We must let students know that as adults we:

- Hear them.
- Take what they are saying seriously.
- Are there to help, coach, and train them.
- Will make sure justice is served.
- Will make them whole again.
- Will hold the aggressor/bully accountable for their actions.
- Will be there to help them in the future.

Eradicating Bullying: Is It Possible? . . . I Say, "Yes!"

When we sit down with our children before the start of a new school year to discuss their goals in school, we do not say, "Let's try for Cs across the board." We encourage and motivate them to strive for all "A's." We acknowledge it will be tough, and it will require a lot of hard work, but nonetheless, we work for the best possible outcome. Subsequently, when it comes to bullying, I encourage all institutions to take a stand and declare their initiative to eradicate bullying. We are not in the business of "dealing" with bullying, we are in the business of not allowing it to exist in our environment. So how do we eradicate it?

ERADICATE (VERB: I'RADI͵KĀT)

Destroy completely; put an end to
Synonyms: eliminate, get rid of, remove, obliterate.
To eradicate bullying we must do two *things:*

1. Train parents, staff, and children on how to handle bullying when it happens regarding:
    a. How to see it.
    b. How to immediately address and remove it.

2. Create an environment so rich in "positives" that bullying would never have a chance to even enter the environment by doing the following:
   a. Set goals and expectations that everyone be kind, respectful, and inclusive.
   b. Share your goals with others (colleagues, supervisors, and so on).
   c. Motivate effectively so those involved want to exceed your expectations.
   d. Get buy-in from your staff (have each person be a contributor at your goal setting meeting so they feel a connection to the mission).
   e. Get buy-in from your children/students/campers and parents (have your staff facilitate the goal setting meeting the same way you led the meeting with them).
   f. Never let your guard down and never give up on this mission.
   g. Celebrate your accomplishments (Celebrations at home can be extra story time, special outing with a parent, and so on. Celebrations at school or camp can be a dance, carnival, game the children want to play, and so on)!

I was known for saying, at my previous camp director job, "I would rather lose one mean camper from our actions, than lose a single camper due to the actions of one mean camper." These are strong words to stand by, but parents, staff, and campers knew I meant business, and therefore no one in our environment would stand up for acts of meanness. As a result, campers felt safe and encouraged to try new things without fear of rejection, humiliation, or being put down.

The result is a community in which people are free to fail, and therefore more likely to learn, due to the supportive environment provided by *everyone*. I believe the above holds true for classrooms in our schools today.

FOLLOW THROUGH

All too often institutions have a great method for handling bullying, but they tend to forget one of the most critical steps of them all, FOLLOW THROUGH. If we fix a car that is leaking motor oil, we can't assume it is fixed forever, we check the source of the leak as time goes by. We make sure there is nothing dripping from the area we fixed, and we make sure there are no new leaks. If there are more leaks, or the same area we fixed leaks again, we take it back to the shop to be fixed again. A customer should leave the shop feeling like he/she has been encouraged to come back if there is another problem. It is much the same way when working with children. They should feel welcomed and encouraged to return by having been provided with feedback that addresses present and future concerns and problems. Every issue must be dealt with or all of our efforts leading into the "fixing/eradicating" of the problem are for naught. So, follow through and follow up often.

Example

My plumber Jamie recently installed a garbage disposal at my house. When he left my house he said, "Keep an eye on it and look for leaks. If you see anything, let me know and I will come back immediately." Jamie is not only an excellent plumber (no leaks) but he made sure I felt comfortable to come back to him in the event of a problem. Even if it is within a year, I will go to Jamie, because I know he cares and stands by his word/work. *Be like Jamie when it comes to working with students who come to you!*

TRAINING

How to See Bullying

- Have appropriate staffing ratios. Give your team a chance to see and hear everything. Not just in the classroom, but on the playing fields at recess, on the buses, and all around.
- Build relationships based on trust. Your team will not see and hear everything that happens, they just can't. So building a relationship of trust will make the victim more inclined to come to you in cases you don't see or hear what happened.
- Promise and follow through on anonymity—children need to know they can trust you, and need to know they won't get in trouble for telling you something.
- Remember this: "Silence is approval" if you see it or it has been reported to you. You must act!

How to Address It and Remove Bullying

- Handle each situation with "kid gloves."
- Take what a child shares seriously, and remember that if *you* think it is a small deal, it is likely a big deal to the person reporting the incident to you.
- Remove the child who was victimized and listen to their story with compassion and concern, let them know you are there to help him/her. And let the student know that you're proud they came to you! You want to encourage this action and therefore must provide positive reinforcement for this behavior.

- Remove the aggressor from the situation and have a one-on-one.
- Remember that perception is reality. While you might get conflicting stories, you need to listen carefully and find the right balance to help both parties come to terms and own their actions/decisions.
- Follow the apology training flowchart to ensure proper accountability, training, and empowerment.
- Communicate with home! Parents are there to help raise their child and need to be in the know.

CREATING

Create an Environment So Rich in the Positives

If you go to your doctor and you learn you have high cholesterol, you have a few options to help your situation. You can improve your diet, or you might take medicine, or be more active. Each of these steps, like the bully-response plan above, is reactionary. What if you took the steps to ensure you never had high cholesterol in the first place? What if you ate well and exercised your entire life? You are ahead of the game and might never know life with high cholesterol!

Remember that bullying is part of human nature and what we are trying to do is to be counter-cultural or create a different, more positive cultural habit and habitat. It will take time and patience, but you must succeed! Be a change agent.

Establish Expectations and Rules for Your Group

1. You must have a meeting within the first fifteen minutes of a group coming together for the first time. Any time a new member enters the group you must sit together and review the rules collectively. In this gathering, never dictate the rules—you want buy-in and ownership, you are a facilitator. You can, of course, lead the group to the answers you want by using leading questions (should we be respectful . . .? what should we do when . . .?). The outcome of this conversation must include words with powerful meanings, explanations, and examples like respect, kindness, inclusion, fairness, taking turns, cooperation, good listening, good sportsmanship, and spirit! Solidify this discussion by making a sign, poster, creed, bill of rights . . . you decide. But get everyone in your group to agree to honor this list of rules and expectations. Then, hang it up or carry it with you. If the occasion arises, you might need to reference the list and remind children what we ALL agreed to uphold.

2. Put positive reinforcements in place. Many schools and camps use different models for this, and each is adaptable to a home situation too. Whether filling a jar with marbles for each time a rule is followed, or expectation exceeded or giving a high five; be sure to recognize and celebrate accomplishments!
3. Evaluate your plan—do this on your own as the administrator and do it with your group.
4. Have debriefs and discussions to check "how things are going." Publicly provide positive-based recognition for behaviors you asked for when you see them.

Example: *One day I went up to the softball field and saw two lines formed (partners throwing and catching across the field). The coach told the girls that for every successful catch they made, they got a point for their team. Girls were motivated to not fail at catching. Before they started throwing, I asked the girls to define good sportsmanship and explained that I wanted to see them being good sports during this activity. The second I heard one child say "nice catch" to her teammate, I jumped all over it! . . . I immediately said aloud, "Ooooh! . . . great, good sportsmanship encouraging your teammate!" What followed was inspiring, every single player shouted to their teammate words of encouragement, "Nice catch, ooh . . . good try . . . . you'll get it next time, way to go!"*

The lesson in the scenario you just read is that most of us are innate people pleasers. Tell students what you want, motivate them to exceed your expectations, and then acknowledge them for their efforts and accomplishments. In this softball-catch game example, my praise was all it took to get them to do what I wanted. With younger children you might need to use point systems, sticker charts, games, and other strategies. For more on *Use of Positive Reward Systems* be on the lookout for the article entitled, "Use of Positive Reward Systems." All of this positive reinforcement in the game of "catch" may apply to a classroom setting in any subject area. Offer positives.

What you've been reading comes down to this, you do not tolerate negative behavior and you maintain a ZERO TOLERANCE POLICY for any acts of meanness. You do that and follow the plan above and you will succeed. Is it true that if you demand excellence, you will get excellence? I say, "Set the expectation for excellence, then give the people the tools needed to succeed, properly motivate them to exceed your expectations and watch the magic."

Closing Thoughts: Now, once you have this eradicating bullying system in place, the learning and growth of the individual and classroom community are limitless! You have to believe in this and set the course as the leader in order for it to work. Inspiration and mission setting are important! Passion for a cause is inspiring. Go forth and inspire by being positive role models for your students and others!

Chapter 12

Shared Reading

STRATEGY EXPLANATION

The first word of this strategy, shared, means that it's interactive. Students are fully engaged when experiencing shared reading (SR). Usually a "big book" is used with students sitting around/near this teacher-led reading. However, since these are not popular any longer, a large smart board or computer may be substituted, or a large chart with "enlarged" text. The students are in a small- or large-, or whole-class formats.

The key factor is that the book being used has easy accessibility and visibility. Also of importance is that this strategy is primarily for early readers, whether in the primary grades, lower elementary ones, or ELL students. Most frequently, a piece of children's literature is used in the picture book format. Most importantly, the text chosen must be visible and accessible to all students.

There should be a variety of texts, including different genres, and digital and visual ones. Whichever is utilized, it's important to apply authentic reading experiences and inviting students to join the teacher in reading often. Sharing the teacher's thought processes while demonstrating a skill or strategy is important as well.

The teacher may read the selected book or story or at least portions of it with the students taking turns in reading the story in front of them. Initially, the picture book story is introduced by discussing the title, cover, and author/illustrator. The class or group may share their reaction to the story, make predictions about what is coming next, reference the character traits presented, determining who has these. Page illustrations are for discussion, as they match the text. Story comprehension is a major factor with teacher-designed questions addressing fact-based literal portions of the text. There may also be applying the story context to one's own life or making suppositions about what the story doesn't directly say but implies.

Story Excerpt Example: Elementary Grade or ELL

Sue led the line from the school bus on the class trip that was visiting the local zoo. When everyone got off the bus, all looked around at the animals. What was soon discovered is that the lions, tigers, giraffes, aquarium animals, such as seals and dolphins, and then zebras, rhinoceroses, and other animals were placed in separate sections, as opposed to being all together. "Hmm," Sue wondered, "where would the horses be?"

Literal Questions: What vehicle took the class to their visiting place? Where was the class visiting on this trip? *Applied Question*: How would you feel about going on a class trip with Sue's class? *Implied Question*: Where would the elephants be kept at the Zoo?

Since the questions are directed toward the entire group, the pressure to answer questions is lessened, as volunteers are sought. The group is "sharing" the reading experience and benefits from that sharing. Discussions may occur as a particular portion of a story is addressed. This portion could include the setting, characters, events, and if present, a story's problem, and solution. Another component of this strategy is that the students may be given the opportunity to construct a different ending to the story. Explanations of their reasoning may be applied as comparisons and contrasts to these "story closing" ideas.

READ-ALOUD IN SR

Author's Note: The teacher may read to the students a portion of the book. When that happens or when the students read there is to be emphasis on vocal tone, facial expressions, voice modulation, and gesturing. The overall ideas are to have students discover the book's content, read the book aloud, discuss the story contents, and then revisit the book after the groups or class has read the book. One other factor about S.R. is that students, although in a group, may have thinking for themselves, hear other's ideas, and compare and contrast these to their own thoughts. This process is part of the Beginning Awareness on the Hierarchal and Reciprocal Reading Chart. Clearly, more skills are seen in practice than the other phases. Look back and see what ones you can observe.

Ultimately, a good deal of interaction occurs when using this strategy. And there is continual reading aloud, which is actually called a "Read-aloud." It models fluent and expressive reading and assists in developing comprehension and critical thinking skills. These have been addressed in the chapter with the chart. Also, students may have a read-aloud without interruption with teacher's observation being the key factor for realizing how the class and/or individual students are performing. Vocabulary increases with practice in pronunciation, visual modality preference evidenced, and talking about story sequencing: What do you think will happen next and why? What are story clues and pictures to help you anticipate the next portion of the story?

SR provides for different genres of books. And there are opportunities for authentic reading experiences with invitations to join the teacher in this collaborative experience. Since the teacher is part of the sharing, this is truly a whole-class experience. Furthermore, the opportunity to participate is continually present in this interactive instructional strategy.

The book is read aloud, and the text may be used for context clues, introduction of new vocabulary, the aforementioned comprehension, scope and sequence, parts of speech, role-playing of a story section, and use of oral expression with voice modulation, intonation, and articulation. Most often, the teacher selects what to emphasize in using this strategy. Observation of the students regarding the reading process is a key factor along with practice reading.

One more thing is that since this is a group sharing activity or may be whole class, there is a natural accommodation necessary for those processing style persons who like to work in this format—an informal room design. Still, since the lesson has structure, and a detailed process for disseminating information, those who enjoy organization are most adept at this style of reading. They do not wait to the last minute to do things, and so those inclined to be analytic are a natural for this strategy. However, the presence of sound, formal or informal room arrangement, not working alone but in partnerships or small groups, and then working on a project to completion relate that SR is suited to most students regardless of the way they process information.

THREE STAGES OF SR

1. Have the students gather around a chart board or smart board. On this presentation device is a story of your choosing. As stated earlier, this strategy is primarily for elementary level students or ELL ones. A children's picture book is most often used for this strategy. The reading material level of difficulty will depend on those in the group. Regardless, there are three stages of presentation for this strategy. The first is what happens prior to the lesson. It is here that the teacher stimulates a discussion about the soon-to-be presented story.

The teacher may use the cover illustration of the reading material to encourage conversation primarily about the book or story topic. Such questions as,

"What do you think is the topic of this book? Or, based on the cover page illustration and title, what's your prediction about what will happen in this story?" The first reading of the story is usually for enjoyment.

2. During the reading of the story, the teacher may address vocabulary by asking for meanings of words. Oral reading of the story is continually evidenced. Actually, you, as the teacher and guide, decide what you want the class to focus on when using the SR strategy. So, focusing or calling attention to specific portions of the text is evidenced.

Perhaps you would like the students to reflect on the topic and ascertain if there is a connection to if from their personal experience. If so, be sure to ask what this connection is and how the use of memory impacts recalling. [Please look at the lesson plan to see what's an idea you may use for your lesson.]

3. Following the application of this reading strategy comes a review of it with the teacher reiterating questions. The teacher also discusses whether predictions made at the onset of reading were or were not realized in the story content. One may have a thorough retelling of the story in one's own words. Questions of the applied and implied comprehension nature are most viable, as these rely on in-depth thinking and become part of prior knowledge for a future SR experience.

ADDITIONAL COMPONENTS OF SR

Echo Reading: Since this is a group experience, the teacher may read a section aloud and then have the students copy the teacher's style of delivery demonstrating flow of the sentences. This process is oftentimes referred to as "echo reading." Another component, if so desired to use, is having the class read a few sentences together.

Choral Reading: This "choral" reading allows for those who have minimal confidence to practice their reading skills when reading alone. Also, this form of reading brings the class together in the "community".

Read Aloud: Reading aloud comes where students are observant of the enlarged version of a book. This allows them to share their reading competencies with the goals of student enjoyment, participation with students doing the reading, and classroom discussion about the text with the teacher is determining the text points of importance based on students' needs.

The teacher makes frequent pauses to ask students open-ended questions calling for opinions. Also, a story context review will enable asking literal comprehension questions about the story. Perhaps, the teacher may cover words with a blank piece of paper and ask, "What is the missing word?"

WHO BENEFITS FROM THIS STRATEGY AND WHY

Since most reading strategies have structure, you can see that students benefit from this strategy in relation to their needs as readers. Here are some advantages to this reading strategy. See how many you can select as you need when you begin reading or you observe now as an educator.

SR allows for tracking print from left to right and word by word with the opportunity for making predictions and inferences about the text being shared. Then again, one of the largest advantages of this strategy is for classroom community-building opportunities. Because of the "sharing" in a group for this strategy, the students are not in individual competition. They are a part of a community through discussion, freedom to express ideas, and realizing that opinions, thoughts, and ideas are relevant to establishing this community of learners. Subsequently, those who enjoy student engagement have an advantage when SR is experienced. And those who are not proponents of this strategy, there is given an opportunity for self-efficacy and acceptance from classmates. Let's not forget there's the benefit of sequencing the story.

The active engagement component is important, as students are not passive recipients of information but form it themselves. As a reading teacher for many decades, this author supports this reading strategy as it offers sustenance for struggling readers or those new to reading through *group work and active engagement*, with respect to all modalities being in-play/evidenced. The "community" with everyone getting the same questions to ponder with support from the book displayed in front of the group or class, also assists those having difficulty reading. If you're wondering how that's possible, then note that the group provides a safe and caring shared environment of readers who feel free to share what they recognize. This is done without rejection. Why? Because they are sharing the reading experience collectively.

By asking questions during the reading and recap of the story, the students are exposed to varied types of comprehension (literal, applied, and implied) that enhance their knowledge of vocabulary, sentence structure, paragraphing, and scope and sequence of the book. They recognize letters and sounds with the oral presentation. This SR strategy uses auditory, visual, tactile, and kinesthetic modalities throughout each session.

Those students requiring feedback have it immediately from the teacher or groupmates along with the story review. What one person forgets another one will pick up in sharing. That factor allows for added comprehension and use of memory and triggers them too. In turn, the students are likely to develop confidence when working with others and may readily transfer this to other stories read alone or with classmates or friends, and at home. Of further importance is that the predictability of the text can build sight word awareness and acuity, which lead to fluency in reading. Thus, those students in need of these skills benefit from SR.

LESSON PLAN FOR SR

Motivation

The teacher hands each student a picture illustration from the book to be read. Each of these cards has a statement on it. The students are to read their cards and determine if the statement appears to be a beginning, middle, or end of story happening. The student's line-up in front of a large piece of paper on the wall that says, Beginning, Middle, End and determine where the statement belongs.

The students read their cards aloud, and the class, with teacher supervision, states if the person is in the right line or not. This kinesthetic involvement also calls for thinking in the form or reflection and projection, which are metacognitive processes. Comparing and contrasting are evidenced, which are beginning thinking actions, along with realizing what card they have, and classifying it. Initial decision-making is evidenced with students' sharing ideas for card placement. That's a critical and creative thinking skill in practice.

LESSON DIRECTIONS AND OBJECTIVES

Using an illustrated story printed on large chart paper or, if available, a classroom smart board, the class will gather around the chosen medium format. The teacher will have selected a children's picture book for this particular lesson. The cover title and illustration will give clues as to what the book addresses. *The students will observe the book and give their thoughts on the book's topic. Next, the teacher will read the sentences of the first page, and then the students will do the same thing with teacher assistance, if necessary. This process continues until the book is read.*

Activities with Questions

1. The students will listen as the teacher reads the first page of the book. They will then read this as a group with students taking turns reading. *(What do you think is the topic of this story? Who are the characters?*

How do you know this? What are the picture clues that help you predict about the present or forthcoming pages of this book?)

2. The students, having seen that this is a rhyming book, also note that the last word of the second stanza is missing. Reading the page, they will use context clues and rhyme to fill in the type of animal the poem is describing. *(What are rhyming words? What are the rhyming words of the first stanza of this poem? What does this first stanza tell us about the animal being described? What are the rhyming words of the second stanza? What does the context tell you this animal type may be? How do you suppose the rhyme and context clues help you decide? What do you suppose is the name of the animal that goes in the blank space?)*
Example:

> There is an animal in the woods.
> It is covered with fur.
> The color is brown but could be black.
> Its name is . . . well, I'm not sure.
>
> I know it's not a lion, and
> I know that its growl scares.
> I think it likes to eat honey.
> Yes, this is a grizzly _____ [bear]

3. The students read the remaining pages of the book and continue to use the clues and rhyme to fill in the missing animal. Then, working in partnerships, the students draw a picture of the animal that goes with the context clue and rhyme. These pictures will be put on display in the classroom or photographed and put on the computer to go with each page's poem. *(What medium are you using for our drawing and why? What is the first animal you drew? What were some characteristics of this animal? Did you know about this animal before you saw and read the book? If so, how did you know this and, if not, why not?)*
4. Again, working with a partner, the students will be given an animal's name. They may use the internet to find a picture of this animal. However, the focus of this activity is to create a two-stanza rhyming poem about this animal. Either the first and third ending lines, or the second and fourth lines have the rhyming word. *(What animal's name did you get? What do you know about this animal? Is it friendly to people or not? How do you know? What are some rhyming words you could use to describe this animal? What lines have you chosen to end with rhyming words?)*

Example:

> I saw this animal last week
> It was standing at the zoo.
> The animal was very large and tall
>
> And had fan ears, unlike me and you!
> It also had a trunk and tusks.
> It was quiet and didn't pant.
> Its legs were tall like trees.
> I knew it was an _____ [elephant]

5. The students will share their poems with the class and ask classmates to use the context clues, as well as rhyme, to discover the animal's name. *(What is a context clue? What is rhyming poetry? What do you think were the key words to help identify your animal's name? What were the rhyming words, and in what lines did they occur? How many people could identify your animal by your clues and/or rhymes? Why do you think this was evident? Did you enjoy this activity? Why or why not?)*

DIFFERENTIATION OF INSTRUCTION

Using the students' poems, they will work in partnerships and attach self-made drawings of their animals. Or the students may find pictures of their animals on the internet and have them accompany their poems. These poem pages pictures will be put together in a class book. Another idea is, instead of making a class book, the students may put their poems and the accompanying pictures or drawings on a class-designed bulletin board.

ASSESSMENT

Using a teacher-made Tally Sheet, the students will evaluate their own poems and those of classmates for content, rhyme, and context clues. They will title each poem with the animal's name. The evaluation will use a Likert scale of highly agree, agree, somewhat agree, and disagree. The scale will address thoughts and opinions of the work presented. A few examples would be, *Did the poem describe an animal? Was the presentation clear? Why or why not? Were you able to identify the context clues? If so, what was one and if not, why do you think that happened? What were the rhyming words in the poem?*

CHARACTER COUNTS AND SEL

Using the poems and accompanying illustrations of the animal in the poem, the students will form groups of three partnerships These partnerships will bring their context-clue poems and animal pictures to other classes in the school. This is done to illustrate their comprehension of these two factors from the SR lesson plan and to share the reading! This exercise is for enjoyment of guessing the animal names and bringing about extended community.

This sharing brings about a school-wide community. The students will invite the classes to add to the poems with rhyme, or create a book of their own, using classroom objects for the poems. These may be such things as a desk, chair, lights, and other classroom furniture or computers and learning devices. The word missing does not need to name the object but must use rhyme and context clues. An example follows:

> I sat at this in the morning.
> And again, in the afternoon
> I didn't use it in the evening.
> Or outside of the classroom
>
> It has 4 legs, a back and seat.
> It's used every day you see.
> This is a piece of furniture.
> It's a desk-chair for you and _____

FINAL THOUGHTS

Regarding the benefits of this SR strategy, Fountas and Pinnell (2020) state that it:

- "Provides enjoyable, successful experiences with print for all students.
- Promotes the development of all aspects of the reading process.
- Builds language skills and enhances vocabulary.
- Provides opportunities to engage in expressive, meaningful, fluent reading.
- Builds understanding of various types of texts, formats, and language structures.
- Build a community of readers."
- *"Shared reading enables all children, regardless of their reading levels, to have enjoyable literacy opportunities every day."—Irene C. Fountas and Gay Su Pinnell:* www.fpblog.fountasand*pinnell.com*

Chapter 13

Guided Reading

Joseph Aurilla, Danielle Bruno, and Alessia Giliberti

STRATEGY EXPLANATION

Guided reading (GR) is an instructional approach that involves a teacher working with a small group of students who demonstrate similar reading behaviors. This is a *leveled* reading program. As such, students are working in groups related to their ability level. "This refers to the general expectation of student performance and competency at a given grade and/or age. Student learners may function at what has been determined as above, at, or below grade level. The actual titles of levels or stages of reading are, Emergent, Early, and Fluent" (Schiering, 1999–2023).

Emergent Reader: Enjoys listening to stories and can retell them, likes writing, and understands that it's the print that has the message of the writer, uses pictures as clues, easily knows to go from left to right in word sequence, knows the difference between beginning, middle, and end of a story, can decode words, uses beginning memorization of a familiar book, and finds words relating to environment, such as tree and grass, finger pointing, recognize word repetition.

Early Reader: Enjoys listening to stories, chooses to read independently, appears confident in sharing thoughts and feelings about books, is able to retell longer stories in sequence, reflects well on story characters, events, and messages of the literary piece, anticipates language and checks it through rereading, brings personal experiences to intertwine with the story, recognizes context clues, relies on pictures and text lines for information, and gains meaning from the text being read.

Fluent Reader: Enjoys listening to long stories, may have a propensity for chapter books, will decide to select books where there is checking and cross-checking language clues, anticipates reading challenges and accepts them, is able to summarize a story, contributes regularly as in Shared Reading guidelines, is a critical reader, shows interest in vocabulary, reads daily, looks for word and sentence meanings, and semantics of words, can retain read material, proofreads writing, and can recall a story in detail.

When making comments about this reading strategy one should offer a specific point or two. So, specifically, there's a need to know that for the student their achievement level in reading may vary from one discipline to another. Hmm, that means that, while in the same grade or age grouping, students may have different ability levels. How does the teacher know about one's ability? Well, determining differences in ability levels is often facilitated through scores on standardized tests. These serve as the determining factor for what is considered "on level" and what is above or below it. Then again, if you've had some experience teaching, observation of reading readiness and aptitude may likely be obvious, so you'll know what the reading level best suited to the student may be (Schiering, 2011). Adapted versions of the same text serve as the mainstay for this reading strategy.

BEFORE, DURING, AND AFTER GR

The key elements for GR are, before reading discussion, independent reading, and after reading discussion. The general goal is to assist students with reading and then get them to work independently. In that vein, it's good to know that this strategy was formed by Vygotsky's 1978 Zone of Proximal Development and Bruner's 2021 notion of students following stages or learning in a continuous process. The practice of GR is based on the belief that the optimal learning for readers occurs when they are assisted by an educator, or expert 'other', to read and comprehend a text with clear but limited guidance.

The teacher's role in GR is to determine what group is best for each student. Then this individual keeps a Runny Record, Reading Conference notes, and an anecdotal record of each student's performance in each group. Of course, each student has a copy of the text to be read and read aloud, as well as silently.

BENEFITS OF GR AND WHY

There are times when readers are afraid to read. Afraid? Why would that be? This author, not learning to read until nearly fourth grade, was terrified when called upon to read. She couldn't speak. Some classmates smiled because they knew she wouldn't try to read aloud, others were silent. However, this GR strategy takes that fear of reading into consideration and provides non-threatening reading instruction, as students are recognized for their strengths in reading. The students are provided a means to succeed. As a result, students develop their aptitude to work independently. Two major benefits of GR are that this strategy works well for students who like working in a small-group format and feel secure in that environment. *It's also good for allowing students to practice reading passages that are designed to meet their reading level.*

Primarily, being at one's reading level is possible with Guided Reading. This is because the group that students are in is made up of those that have similar or the same reading skills. GR provides for those components in the Balanced Literacy strategy with Shared Reading, Reader's and Writer's Workshop, Independent Writing and Reading, Word Study, and Read Aloud being parts of the G.R. framework. In a way, this strategy allows such a variety of thinking and feelings that it's suited to all classroom members. Overall, GR provides students with a feeling of being confident in their reading because of the teacher's attention to students' needs, which are determined by their skill sets.

With respect to how one processes information, this strategy is well suited for those who like structure, and benefit from teacher assistance. Ultimately, G.R. is important and to students' advantage because it gives them the chance to apply the strategies they already know to a new text. The teacher provides support while the goal is independent reading, with student confidence. That accomplishment is the "why" of choosing G.R.

Independent Reading reflects the reader's preferred reading material and may be done for information or pleasure. Such things as magazines, fiction and non-fiction books, informational books, as well as those involving history, whether fictionalized or not, are those genres that a reader may choose. Subsequently, that choice idea allows for creativity in selection of material. And choices may involve any classroom discipline.

Now that you've seen some benefits for students using this G.R. strategy, here are a few more: Support for readers in their processing competencies, responsive student teacher interaction, support of the readers' active engagement in a variety of texts and topics, as selected by student interest, ability level, learning style preferences, and pace, develop thinking skills (refer to the Chart), and time on task. GR provides opportunities for students to use pictures as a source of information, use the first and closing letters of a word and involvement in discussion, with an exchange of information about the topic of the book. Finally, there is continual evident student success as challenging texts are available to them, and as one becomes proficient at one level, one moves on to another, higher one.

GR COMPONENTS: BEFORE, DURING, AND AFTER

1. Before reading, the teacher accesses the prior knowledge of the topic of the reading to be done when the group meets. Let's say the topic of reading is one that calls attention to students' interest areas. Relating these in a small group sharing calls attention to the story to be read or the passage the teacher has designed. As these interest areas are expressed, the teacher records them.
2. The students predict the material to be read, and the teacher notes these for similarities and differences. The group is therefore determining what's to be read, as well as using the cognitive skills of realizing, comparing, and contrasting the interest areas, analyzing these in a group discussion, and evaluating what's to be learned by reading the provided passage. The teacher assists with vocabulary, and ideas presented in the text as seen through reflection on one's own experiences. Also involved are word-solving strategies and analysis of sound-letter relationships and word parts.
3. The teacher, having read the material prior to meeting the groups, sets the scene by briefly summarizing the story plot. Stories or books selected are to deal with areas of interest to the students or are part of a societal commonality. Problem-solving and decision-making may be added components of this strategy's third step with analysis of the story being read. Meaningful conversations, including asking questions between the teacher and the group, are important for continual guidance regarding what's being read.

Lesson Plan: *This Lesson Plan* (Schiering, 2023) *is based on the research of this chapter's authors,* Joseph Aurilla, Danielle Bruno, and Alessia Giliberti.

The story from chapter 16 titled "The Howling Cat and Love," by Sue Nauman, is used for this Lesson Plan. The story is for the fluent reader. Adaptations have been made to show a few paragraphs at each level. Please note the increase in the number of words from one reading level to the next.

Explanation: Leveled reading books exist, but not having permission to use copyrighted material, this author adjusted the story in chapter 16 of this book. If you were doing GR in a classroom, you would have GR textbooks to utilize for any given lesson. The teacher decides, as previously explained, who goes in which group for reading that matches student's abilities.

Lesson objectives:

1. *The students are to read silently the story presented to them using their silent reading skills.*

2. *The students will share, with teacher guidance, the main idea of the story and its meaning, including identification of characters and events in the story.*
3. *The students, working in group format, with or without the teacher's assistance, will answer the questions following the story for an in-depth review of the reading passage.*
4. *The students, working in partnerships, will write a new ending to the story to share with the class at the next day's reading time.*

Author's Note: What follows are three "Levels" or "Stages" of the same story. This story content, for the most part, was retrieved from this book's chapter 16. It's the story titled *My Howling Cat with Love*. In actuality, GR stories are longer than what's presented on the next few pages. This author shortened or lengthened the first paragraphs to allow you, the reader, to see the difference in difficulty regarding material that had the basic information but got progressively more advanced in GR's leveled-by-ability reading. The questions remain the same, as stated in the Objective of the lesson, but they may be teacher-modified to match the reading level of the students in their assigned groups.

A few words are *emboldened* in each story to be recognized as the main vocabulary words. When detailed questions for each excerpt are designed, the students are asked about these words and then find more descriptive words in the paragraphs. This task is done within the group format with teacher assistance.

As you read the paragraphs at each level, you will easily see the passages becoming more difficult. Each passage excerpt is designed to assist the reader in determining the main idea, characters, and actions of the story's beginning.

LEVEL 1

One Saturday morning when living in Yavapai Hills, I was sitting in my *nice* house at my desk working at the computer. I saw a blur of an animal go up the tree very quickly. I wondered what it was when I looked out the window. There on the ground, was a coyote looking menacingly up the tree. "What was in the *big* tree that the coyote was viewing so intently?

I *hurried* to the front door and opened it, and saw my cat, Isis, at the top of the tree. She looked scared, and her head was bent down to see if the coyote was going to climb the tree. Isis was *straddling* two flimsy branches, which were swaying back and forth under her heavy weight. The next thing I knew, the coyote was gone. But Isis hung on to the tree branches and wasn't moving from them. (156 words)

Chapter 13

LEVEL 2

One very sunny Saturday morning when I was in Yavapai Hills, Arizona, I was sitting in my *nice* cozy house at my large black desk. I was working at the computer. I saw a blur of an animal go up the tree very quickly. I wondered what it was when I looked out the window. There on the ground was a coyote looking up the tree. I thought, "What was in the *big* tree that the coyote was viewing so intently? I think it is my cat. I had to find out if this was true.

 I *hurried* to the front door and opened it, went out on the porch, and there was my cat, Isis, at the top of the tree. She looked scared, and her head was bent down to see if the coyote was going to climb the tree. Isis was *straddling* two flimsy branches, which were swaying back and forth under her heavy weight. My cat was very large for her age of one year. She was larger than any of the cats I'd ever had before her. Maybe I overfed her. The next thing I knew, the coyote was gone. But Isis hung on to the tree branches and wasn't moving from them. (209 words)

LEVEL 3

One very sunny and hot Saturday morning I was in Yavapai Hills, Arizona, I was sitting in my *nice* comfortable and cozy house at my large black marbled desk. I was working intently at the computer. I was very focused and liked working uninterrupted. But I saw a blur of an animal go up the tree quickly. I wondered what it was. Then, I looked down out the large unshaded window. There on the ground was a coyote looking up the tree. I thought, "What was in the *big* overpowering tree that the coyote was viewing so intently?" In my mind my response was "I think it is my cat. I had to find out if this was true. So much for uninterrupted computer time. While I was working so steadfastly on my assignment from school, this situation was well worth my immediate attention."

 Subsequently, I *hurried* to the front door and opened it. Then I went out on the screened-in porch. I looked up as best as I could, and there was my large cat, Isis. She was at the top of the overpowering tree. She looked scared, and her head was bent down to see if the coyote was going to climb the tree. Isis was *straddling* two flimsy branches, which were swaying back and forth under her heavy weight. My cat was very large for her age of one year. She was larger than any of the cats I'd ever had before her. I thought, "Maybe I'm overfeeding her." The next thing I knew the coyote was gone. But Isis hung on to the tree branches and wasn't moving from them. (271 words)

Author's Note: Each version of the story provides more detail sentences than the previous one. That change allows the leveled reading concept to be visualized. Now the questions that come from the read version will be more difficult, because of the complexity of the story being read. While the questions and new ending are based on the entire story and you are only provided a sample here, you're invited to look at chapter 16's accounting. So, you will see how the story ended and can evaluate with the information given how the students are working on level.

ACTIVITIES FOR A GR LESSON

These questions in italics after each activity may be addressed in each leveled GR group.

1. Following the teacher's offering context to the story, the students will independently read the story. *(What was the topic of the story? Was it easy to find this? Why or why not? How did the main character feel about her cat? Of what do you suppose the cat was afraid? Is this something that would frighten you? Why or why not?)*
2. The students will read the story for meaning, taking turns in a group read. Then, upon completion of the reading, the students will reflect and share their opinions of the story. This is done while calling attention to their perception of the story's problem. *(Do you prefer to read silently or in a group? Why? What was your overall opinion of the story? What was the main problem presented early in the story?)*
3. The students will design and then answer group-mates' questions to get the most information about this howling cat, that they can from their version of the story. Some of these questions will likely include, "Why is the cat in a tree? Why is the cat howling? What was the cat's owner initially doing? Why did she move away from her assignment? What sort of situation was the cat in when it climbed the tree? What role did the coyote play in this story? What did the coyote do, and did this solve the story problem? Why or why not?
4. Remaining in small groups, the students will use the creative writing technique and create a new ending to the story. The ending must be positive and show assistance. The students will then share their analysis of the story's new ending. *(After discussing with your group mates a possible ending to this story, what three do you have? How are these positive endings? How would you help your pet or a person who was in danger?)*

Assessment with Existing and Additional Story Questions: These are for all groups with teacher-led discussion and/or personal response with only group members. The answers to the questions will determine the students' comprehension of the story, as well as their ability to address the scope and sequence of the story and answer applied and implied comprehension questions: *(1) What are the topics of the story? (2) Where does the story writer live? (3) What is the setting of the story? (4) What is the main idea of the story? (5) Do you think living on a hillside means the character is far from other houses? (6) Why or why not? (7) Who are the characters in the story? (8) What animal is the key figure in the story? (9) Where was the writer sitting? (10) What type of animal is the lead character? (11) What kind of sound did the author use to describe how fast the cat traveled up the tree? (12) How was the coyote looking at the cat, and what is a descriptive word for that character? (13) There were four bold-letter words. (14) These were nice, big, hurried, and straddling. (15) These are adjectives, and what does each of the emboldened vocabulary words mean? (16) Why are these words important to story comprehension? (17) What are other descriptive words (adjectives) you found in this story? (18) What are ones you could add to offer more detail?*

DIFFERENTIATION OF INSTRUCTION: PRESENTATION OF STORY ENDINGS: WHOLE GROUPS TO THE WHOLE CLASS

Using the basic content and context of the story, the students worked in whole group format to create a new and positive ending to the story. The students will now share these story endings. After each ending is presented, the class will discuss the new endings and present their thoughts, ideas, opinions, and feelings about these new endings. The format for an oral presentation, as seen earlier in this book, should be applied.

CHARACTER COUNTS AND SEL

Using the GR strategy provides ample opportunities for class members to converse with one another. And to write a new story ending. This process calls for collaboration, metacognitive thinking, and critical and creative cognition. When these factors take place, the class is engaged in SEL by virtue of the assignment. Partnership work and having the teacher as part of groups by guiding the reading and writing further promote good character.

Interestingly, the final activity of creating a positive new story ending furthers exhibition of character formidable traits and produces constructive,

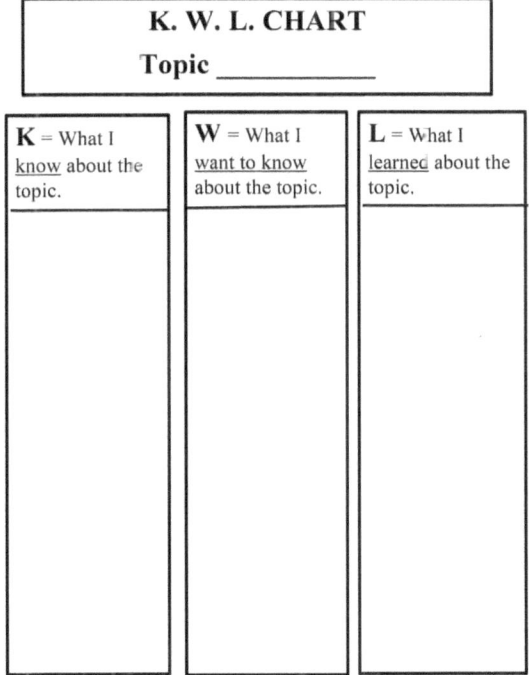

Figure 13.1 KWL Chart. *Source*: Schiering, 1976.

practical, and helpful responses. Then too, story building allows for expression of feelings that create comfort and harmony by being positive.

EXTENDING THE LESSON WITH A KWL CHART

This KWL Chart is a whole class activity and brings about communication that delves into what is helpful about the story or the topic, what wants to be known, and what has been learned. This review of the story serves as a point for additional comprehension. However, the "what wants to be learned" allows for expanded thinking on the topic of the story. This thinking may carry over to other characters or how one acts in a stressful situation, such as the one the cat was experiencing.

Lastly the question about what was learned may address the actual story or story's new ending and expose the class to an expansion of their thinking. What one learns from a story may not be what another has learned. This sharing brings about further comprehension of classmates' thinking and emotions.

Chapter 14

Balanced Literacy's Independent Writing

BALANCED LITERACY BACKGROUND AND INDEPENDENT WRITING STRATEGY EXPLANATION

The Balanced Literacy (BL) strategy is a combination of reading and writing and includes several different ways to teach these. Most explicitly, BL involves Read Aloud, Shared Reading, Guided Reading, Independent Reading, Write Aloud, Shared and Interactive Writing, Experiential Read Aloud, Choral and Echo Reading, Guided Writing, and Independent Writing. You may question why there are so many different methods of reading and writing. Well, they simply provide students with a wide variety of experiences to find one that best suits their needs.

Thus far in this book either through reading strategies or the activities presented in lesson plans, most of BL has been addressed. What is presented now is a mini- or abbreviated version of this section on Independent Writing. This strategy provides a chance for students to realize their ability to write with little teacher intervention. Students at any grade level may address topics of interest to them and research information on that topic in advance of doing their writing.

With this strategy, students comprehend that there are stages of writing which include planning, revising, and editing their work before having a final product. Additionally, Independent Writing addresses writing styles such as (Schiering, Spring 2022: OLLI Short Story Curriculum):

1. Essay,
2. Persuasive,
3. Cause and effect,
4. Biographies or autobiographies,

5. Magazine articles,
6. Reporting an actual historic event with real or fictionalized characters,
7. Problem and solution,
8. Interviews,
9. Comparing and contrasting, and
10. Writing from different perspectives (first, second, or third person).

OTHER FORMS OF WRITING WITH EXAMPLES (SCHIERING, SPRING 2022: OLLI SHORT STORY CURRICULUM)

A. ***Sensory/Descriptive:*** This type of writing presents a picture in words. An example would be: The beautiful dog ran through the thick woods in wild abandon. The young boy followed the dog but walked slowly and cautiously. The grandfather stood by the edge of the woods waiting for the two to emerge. The grandmother yelled to her husband to enter the woods and look for the dog and the boy. The wind howled as a storm was approaching. One could feel the thickness of the air, smell the moisture of an about to happen rain, and hear the leaves fluttering in the trees.

B. ***Practical/informative:*** This type of writing presents basic information in a clear manner. An example would be: The car was disabled, and the driver was angry. She stood near the trunk of the car waiting for assistance. However, when one hour had passed, she became more disgruntled. Her patience was at the lowest level when a driver pulled over to help.

C. ***Imaginative/Narrative:*** This writing format tells a real or imaginary story. An example would be: Down the road there lived an angel. In the evening, this non-real being danced all over the valley. People saw her in the hours before darkness came and the moon rose. One hot summer day the angel was seen speaking to a ten-year-old boy. This boy was known as the town trickster because of his playful antics. Hmmm, what were they talking about? is what I wondered.

D. ***Analytical/Expository:*** This story type presents an analysis or explanation of something. An example would be: It is important for there to be kindness when speaking to another person. This is because that type of conversation allows one to like conversing and may, as a result, feel good about themselves. Imagine if kindness was the only type of verbal discourse. Wouldn't we then have a lot of happy people? It seems logical that we would have that. Still, I think getting new ideas calls for just a pleasant exchange of information. Maybe that is being kind. All I know is that I love to talk with others in a friendly way.

Of course, being exposed to these varied types of writing (1–10 and A–D) is brought about by exposure to reading material in these areas. The expansiveness of Independent Writing is enthralling.

BENEFITS OF INDEPENDENT WRITING AND WHY

Perhaps one of the biggest benefits of this reading strategy is to have the students put into practice the book's five objectives. Other advantages include time for one to focus on word usage, punctuation, and comparing and contrasting the other writing works to which they have been exposed. Then again there is the opportunity to use technology for accessing multiple meanings of words.

Cognitive Skill Development and Application: High on a list benefitting Independent Writing is students' opportunity to decide on a topic for their writing. So, students will involve the cognitive skills of decision-making, comparing and contrasting, problem-solving, risk-taking, recalling and reflection, sequencing, and self-actuating. Refer to the Hierarchal and Reciprocal Thinking Chart in chapter 1.

Themes: Students also realize themes of a story with emphasis on first locating the topic to be addressed and designing activities for the characters, which include who they will be and how many characters there will be. For that task they will use descriptive writing. And learning an author's point of view is also necessary in theme development.

Topics: There are a variety of these, and here are just a few. Note that some deal with positive character traits, as seen in chapter 16. Subsequently, when these appear, they can be referenced in this book. Topics: growing up, hope, self-image, friends (read Choice in Short Story in chapter 16), trust, happiness and joy or the opposite, prejudice, problems facing society every day such as harassment, bullying, discrimination, nature, time periods in sequence, love, fairness, and patriotism.

Plots: These five stages of story plot development are listed and explained in chapter 5 of this book.

The reason for this Independent Writing strategy as a component of BL is primarily for varied processing style persons. Developing good writers who comprehend how to construct a story is key. Those learners who prefer to work alone and in a quiet space are accommodated. However, so are those who enjoy sharing and collaborating with discussion, *following* the presentation of writing by oneself. Working on a project to completion is evident, and so is multitasking for those who like to work on several projects at the same time. Having a formal room design would benefit those writing in the classroom, but writing could also be done at home in an informal space. Independent Writing's portion of BL is one that accommodates most students one way or another.

LESSON PLAN OBJECTIVES

1. *Following reading Short Stories in part IV of this book, students will be able to write a story of their own.*
2. *The topics will be provided by the teacher who polls the class on what ones they'd like to address. Students will select their topic to write a Short Story.*
3. *When students complete the Independent Writing of a short story, they will share with the class, in an oral presentation, using the Guidelines from chapter 7 of this book.*

MOTIVATION

The students will be read a Short Story titled *The Choice* from chapter 16 of this book. However, this reading will be done as if in a play with the main character having a personal dialogue with herself.

Next, the students will hear the story *Why Were They Laughing* for realization of how to write humor. This story will be acted out, as was the first one. Both presentations will follow the Guidelines for an Oral Presentation, as provided in chapter 7.

LESSON ACTIVITIES

1. The students will listen to the two stories presented by the teacher in the "Motivation" section of this lesson. They will then give their opinions about each story's theme, and what they like or dislike about the story and why. *(What was the theme/main idea of the first story and how do you know this? What were the important words that led you to know the theme? How does the story topic connect to the story's theme? How did you relate to this story? Who were the main characters, and what were their personality traits? What were the main messages of the story?)*

2. After listening to the second read story, *Why Are They Laughing*, the students will hold a classroom discussion about using humor in a story. *(Did you find this story humorous? If yes, to whom was the humor addressed? If not, why not? Which Guidelines for an Oral Presentation were evident? Why do you think these guidelines may be important when speaking in front of a group? How do you think you would present your story to the class? What are some Guidelines you'd be sure to include? Why?).*
3. The students will be assigned to groups of four to read the remaining six stories in the Short Story section (chapter 16) of this book. [If the students are in a classroom that does not have these stories available, the teacher will select stories she wants the class to read.] In these groups, the students will discuss and take notes on the five components of the plot. *(What was the Exposition [characters and setting] of the story you read? What was the topic of the story, and how did this become evident in the Rising Action of the story? What was the Climatic Moment? What was the Falling Action? What was the story's Resolution? What was your overall reaction to the story? Can you see yourself writing a similar story? Explain your answer.)*
4. Having experienced theme, topic, and plot factors of a Short Story, the students will work independently to write a story of their own choosing. *(What is your story topic or main idea? Why do you suppose you selected this topic? What is the theme of your story? What is the Rising Action, and how does this impact your story? What are the Climatic Moments? What is the Falling Action and Resolution that provide the author's message? Is there a subliminal message, along with the overt one, and if so, what is this? How did it feel to be involved in Independent Writing? Explain your answer.)*
5. Over the next few weeks, the students will orally present their stories to the class. They will use the Guidelines for an Oral Presentation, as provided in chapter 7. *(What are the Guidelines you used for presenting your story? Do you think these were effective and why? Do you think others in the class responded well to your topic, and if so, why? How did you feel about presenting your story? Why do you suppose you felt that way? What are two things about Independent Writing that you truly like and why?)*

ASSESSMENT

Prior to Activity 4, the class will be provided with a "Reaction to Story" sheet. On this, the students will write their general reaction to the story and what Oral

Presentation Guidelines they noted being applied. This quasi-evaluation peer review will have the person's name presenting the story, story title, main idea, and the two types of actions for a plot, climatic moment, and resolution. These will be given to the teacher for review. The students may also review their work.

Differentiation of Instruction: Working in small groups, the students will create a round-robin story for pleasure reading and sharing. They will be presenting the story to the class with group members taking turns sharing their portion of the story. The stories are to be on a teacher-assigned topic that addresses community, interest areas of students (pets, sports, vacations, working, future goals, school, community helpers) with each having information on and analysis of character traits.

Be sure to use the Writer's Workshop rules, as seen in chapter 11 in the section titled "How to Use the Writer's Workshop."

CHARACTER COUNTS AND SEL

The stories presented in chapter 16 and read by the teacher and/or class have addressed character traits that are, for the most part, positive. The small group workthat is done with analysis of the stories,provide ample collaboration during this lesson on story, plot and theme. Additionally, students have thinking and feeling responses to the stories to conversationally address. Having the opportunity to write and read aloud each story, the students have further social interaction regarding speaking with one another. This is particularly evident in the small-group work on the round-robin story. Then, the peer review also provides student-to-student interaction with an opportunity to evaluate oneself, and others in the classroom.

EXTENDING THE LESSON

The students will create a "Plot Diagram" for display in the class. This is of their own design, but includes the five steps of their story's plot. These diagrams may be done on the computer and sent as an email to classmates. Or, if not having this technology available, the students will design their diagram on paper and give a copy to each classmate. Another idea is to make a slide or poster of the Plot Diagram for future viewing by the class. A discussion will be held following the presentation of the diagram for classroom community building and future story ideas. The concept of making a diagram prior to writing a story will be explored for structure preceding a writing assignment.

FACTOID

Chapter 14 through this one have focused on strategies that present detailed information about each one represented in this book. You may ask, "Then, why is there this chapter?" Well, so much emphasis on reading leads to a time for writing. Yes, there have been written assignments in Lesson Plans, but Independent Writing has not been part of the collaboration. Let's see what you know up to this point:

1Q. Do you have to be a good reader to be a good writer? Why or why not?
1A. This book's author would answer this question with a "No!" That is because you may well have excellent listening skills that focus on one's recall of the story line and some details. **Good listening equates with good writing as much as does good reading**.
2Q. What are the two different perspectives of writing?
2A. There is the application of different genres in writing. These include but are not exclusive to first person (Writing from the author's perspective) or the third person (someone observing and reporting what's happening in the story). You're asked to refer to the Anecdote chapter 15 or Short Story chapter 16 to see and decide how the writer is presenting the story to the reader. What is the theme of each story in the Sort Story chapter?
3Q. What are some different forms of writing?
3A. Informational pieces like how to make something (chocolate pie, ride a bicycle, behave properly in a classroom). There's retelling stories, using speech balloons, like in cartooning. Also, one could use topic specific by writing in different disciplines, such as math, science, and social studies. Use of story topics in this chapter's lesson plan may be addressed to answer this question.
4Q. What are some reasons to have Independent Writing?
4A. Mainly, this type of writing assists students in becoming proficient by using their imagination and being exploratory. Also, interest areas provide a basic platform to observe one's creativity. Writer's Workshop may precede the students' actual writing. The writer has time to reflect on a topic, or once beginning, story scope and sequence are evident.

Allowing students' time to research a topic is viable for a reason to have this writing format. Finding one's literary voice is a final reason for using this strategy which provides each student the opportunity to present the student's own version of an incident or anecdote.

Author's Note: This author didn't do well in reading in school, or for that matter anywhere else. When she was presented with learning to read, the strategy used was not effective for her processing style or ability at decoding words. So, when she became a writer of children's books and textbooks dealing with teaching strategies, this was, for some, a surprise. What many did not realize was her ability to listen to and think deeply about any subject matter presented, regardless of the grade level.

In fifth grade she began writing stories based on personal experiences. These included falling off her bicycle because her dad let go of the back of its seat. This was when she was seven. Another topic was how her sister knitted her a sweater. With an introduction to poetry and rhyming words, she began writing four verse stanzas. That ability carried over to writing poems that do or don't rhyme. This growth took place from grade five to the present.

Also of note is a teacher's influence on her early and later public-school studies. Reading and writing are two skills focused on in this book. However, this author strongly believes that the demeanor of a teacher impacts all the reading strategies presented in this book. Some accommodations include: (a) choosing a time to read and write, (b) selecting reading materials, (c) building on thinking and feelings skills, (d) assisting pleasantly and positively using instructional strategies, (e) determining time on task, (f) encouraging independent reading and writing, (g) discussing collaboration in an even exchange of thoughts, ideas, opinions, and the two types of feelings, and (h) providing independent reading and writing time with classroom sharing.

MOST IMPORTANTLY

Every grade level class needs time for establishing and building classroom community. This task may be done with the anecdotes and short stories in this text, or in an area of the room for sharing stories developed by using one's imagination. "Constructive Sharing." That is a time to bring the class together, as a community of learners and teachers.

Part IV

TEACHING READING THROUGH ANECDOTES AND SHORT STORIES

Chapter 15

Anecdotes

Persons of Good Character

INTRODUCTION

This chapter is provided for use in any of the six different reading strategies presented in this book. These may be used to stimulate memory, recognition, comparisons, and contrasts to one's own experiences. What one chooses to share shows that the cognitive skills of prioritizing, communicating in oral or written formats, and sequencing are happening simultaneously. Additionally, there's evaluating and analyzing when anecdotes are shared and personal reflections are observed. All of the aforementioned thinking skills are provided along with pleasure reading and conversing back and forth with classmates provides for social-emotional learning with discourse and discussions about the material in this chapter. Additionally, specifically, the anecdotes may be read for pleasure and act as a stimulus for students writing their own anecdotes.

The Purpose

There are several reasons/purposes for including this chapter in this book. The main one is to use these anecdotes for social-emotional learning. An example is provided in the Reciprocal Reading chapter. The second reason is to make students aware, through sharing these positive experiences, that good is noted in many different ways and having students note good things about themselves when they may have demonstrated their character traits. And, naturally, these anecdotes serve for oral presentations.

Perhaps the most effective application of these anecdotes is for the incorporation of role plays in non-discriminate grade levels. This point means that any grade from early elementary through high school and college might use these anecdotes to focus on positive character traits when exhibited. "Exhibited how?" Through role-play scenarios with class members using their tactile and kinesthetic modalities for learning. Role plays may call for the designing of scenes, character analysis, perhaps scenery, and dialogue for acting out the anecdote. What follows are directions for one way to use the anecdotes.

Directions: Anecdotes on Character Traits

If possible, divide the class into groups of six. Each student in the group selects a character trait from the list of international ones (respect, caring, trustworthy, fair, responsible, good citizen). Now, set aside a few minutes for writing about a time when you saw, or you exhibited that trait. Be specific with naming the trait and providing the setting in space and time. Then, give details about the incident regarding who was involved and the sequence of events. Next, share these with the group. Lastly, reconvene the whole class and, as each character trait is named, have a volunteer from each group share their anecdote.

Examples of Anecdotes

My Fourth Grade Teacher

By Alan Gurwitz

Kindness and Caring: In the fourth grade we were studying about the United Nations building. And, as usual, I was doodling instead of paying attention. I didn't realize that the teacher was looking over my shoulder. She definitely noticed that I was drawing. I thought I was in trouble once I noticed she was there. But she surprised me by saying, "That's very nice, Alan."

I was speechless, as I was expecting a reprimand with disgust. What she said next really shocked me as she complimented me on my art ability. Actually, she went a bit further and suggested that, instead of doing the written assignment, I do drawings of the United Nations building and bring them into class. And so, I did. That teacher, Mrs. Turk, recognized that I could draw well, complimented my work, and put my drawings on the bulletin board for display.

This acknowledgment of the UN drawings was followed by her suggestion that next year I take a special art class at our school. This class was offered in the fifth and sixth grades. I followed her suggestion and attended this class where I honed my talent. This class was only graphic arts, my area of concentration the next year as well.

As it turned out, the teacher who taught those classes suggested I apply to the high school of Art and Design in NYC. I did! And I was accepted. Here I excelled in graphic arts and later went on to pursue a career in art.

This initial act of kindness from my fourth-grade teacher, her taking the time to acknowledge and thereby encourage me, was far-reaching for me. Her statements, when I was 10, made all the difference for me in my studies. Sometimes we do not know how being thoughtful might impact another. I can speak only for myself in relating that her initial recognition of my drawings, influenced my entire life.

Kevin's Story

By Peter Lodini

This story takes place in 2001. I'd been on the Police force in my "smallest county in New York State" for thirteen years. Looking back to a few days before 9/11, I felt disgruntled with how much discontent and selfishness surrounded me. It was a "toxic" time. And then, there was this one day when terrorists came to our country and could not be ignored.

What happened was that the World Trade Center in New York City had been flown into by—did it matter whom? In a way, the answer would be yes. But, overall, what happened for me was that I was one of a group of police officers. We were special in that we volunteered to take a Police Van (Old ambulance) to NYC to lend a hand to work on the "pile" of extreme debris.

We were driving down Westside Highway. It was empty other than for first responders and police vehicles. We were the only ones allowed on this roadway. And then there were people everywhere alongside the road. You may question, "What were they doing?" They were chanting "USA, USA" and giving out work gloves and water to all vehicles coming down the road headed to the World Trade Center site.

In that moment, I was moved by humanity and its being there for one another. This was openly a display of affection. In a time of extreme tragedy, we pulled together not just as a community, but also as a nation who cared about one another. I was renewed with the open demonstration of caring. Interestingly, we never made it downtown, as we didn't have clearance. But we waited in the staging area along with those from nearby states. They included Connecticut. We were all joining together for our country, for all those who in an instant lost their lives or loved ones and experienced horror. We joined together with love, caring, and good citizenship to lend a helping hand to those who mattered most in a time of chaos.

Hero

By Julia DiBiase

Kind and Good Citizen: This story took place many years ago when I was a little girl. It was a snowy afternoon as I was driving from New York to Maine, going to ski for the week with my family. It was winter break at school, and my cousins and I were so excited to take a road trip to a big comfy house in Maine. Our two families were in separate cars, following one another until we would get to our destination.

As we traveled further north, the snow began to come down faster, and the temperatures kept dropping. The roads were extremely icy, and our parents drove with great caution. The deeper we got into the mountains, the steeper the roads grew. While looking out the windows, admiring the beautiful scenery, we noticed something horrible had just happened off to the side of the road. Both my father and my uncle Rob pulled over their cars and jumped out to help.

There had been a family traveling whose car flipped over, leaving them trapped inside and trying to get out. There was a mom, dad, little child, and a baby. Fortunately, my dad and uncle were able to pull the family out to safety and have police and an ambulance arrive on scene. While everyone was a little shaken up, the family was safe, and they were so thankful that somebody stopped to help.

I am sure this story is so special to the sweet family that was rescued that day, but the story is just as important to me. My uncle passed away with cancer two short years after this event took place. I was eight years old and did not have many memories of my time spent with him. However, this is a memory of him that I will never forget. He and my father acted in kindness and as good citizens, jumping out of our cars without hesitation to help this family in need. They were someone's hero that afternoon in February and in my eyes, my uncle will forever be remembered as a hero.

The Donut Shop

By David Fisher

Good Citizenship: Over my many years as an adult, I have always enjoyed spending vacations at the Jersey Shore during the summer months. However, the year 2022 was the first time I was there during the winter. My daughter and I were there for our friend's special 50th birthday party. We shared a house with other attendees, on a boardwalk overlooking the beach and ocean. On this particular day, a walk on the boardwalk was met with subfreezing temperatures and high winds. Since it was winter, all the typical warm weather shops and amusements were closed. The main road, running parallel to the beach, also had very few open shops.

We did find a restaurant nearby for lunch and spent an afternoon watching World Cup soccer. While there, we found out that there was a place to get breakfast on the main drive just below us to which we could walk. It was quite small and blended in with closed businesses on either side that we hadn't noticed earlier.

The next morning my daughter and I were up early and, therefore, elected to brave the freezing weather to bring back coffee and breakfast items. The main event of the day was to be our friend's party that night. As it turned out, that freezing morning walk would make the day even more special. The little breakfast store specialized in donuts made to order, with many different toppings from which to choose. They were made as you watched, from batter to finish. All employees were dressed as elves in keeping with the Christmas theme.

As we observed the making of our order, we complimented the manager on the uniqueness of the process. She thanked us and then warned us that she was expecting a large group of children shortly for a Christmas party. And at that moment, in walked one of the best Santa helpers I have ever seen (hmm, or was he a helper?). My daughter even took a selfie with him. The scene was set: Santa; the elves, decorations, delicious smells, and a staff that exuded holiday warmth and excitement. The children and parents began to arrive. The manager told us they expected upwards of 120 people in this small but welcoming place. What she told us next would make this party, in this place, and by these people, even more special.

It turns out that this donut shop is very involved with their community fund drives in support of stopping childhood cancer. During the past year and a half, they sold special bracelets in support of an organization called "Kick Cancer Overboard." This organization provides free cruises to families whose members are battling cancer. Because they sold enough bracelets, they were able to select a local family to receive a cruise to Bermuda. And this would be done as a surprise during the party!

We gathered our donut order and left with smiles on our faces that reflected those of the people in that donut shop. We had witnessed the plans for celebrating the efforts of a generous and caring community. P.S.: The walk back to the house seemed to feel much warmer because of the community that cared about others in and around it. This was a place that represented not just good citizenship but kindness, respect, responsibility, and trust.

Chapter 15

Helping Hands

By Alan Offen

Caring and Trustworthy: My mother passed away in 1980. A few years later, my dad sold the old family residence and moved into an apartment. He was legally blind and alone. I, essentially, was responsible for his care. Although he had Meals on Wheels for weekly meals, which was a Godsend, that left the weekends empty for providing food. Subsequently, providing breakfast, lunch, and dinner became my prime duty.

Every weekend we would go to Fox's Deli for lunch and then to Wegman's grocery store to purchase food for later that day and for Sunday. This went on for approximately ten years. But what if I were out of town for the weekend? Usually if this occurred, I'd be away with my wife. My grandkids were grown and either had moved away or were in college. What then?

Stepping into this gap was my dear friend Brian. He took over in my absence, taking my dad to lunch and Wegmans, listening and (importantly) enjoying my dad's stories. He was the go-to guy. To this day, Brian fondly recalls his time with my father.

During summers, when my daughter Nancy was home from college, many times she would call me and say, "I'll take grandpa; you take a day off form caring for him." These calls were unsolicited and gave me great solace. As I write this, the memory of her calling me and helping with grandpa brings a broad smile to my face. Brian and Nancy, the caring they showed to my dad and trustworthiness they showed to me are a gift that I have appreciated to this day . . . from the bottom of my heart. Bless them!

College Graduate Class

By JoAnn Victor-Fassman

Compassion and Kindness: In nursing, I teach my undergraduate students to use compassion and kindness in caring for others. This is because I believe, from my nursing experiences, that these are essential elements in the direct care of patients. I instruct students to be mindful in utilizing these components of "care" for both patients and others. This is regardless of the time-consuming demands of advancing technology in their documentation of patient care.

What I have discovered is that, both in the classroom and the clinical setting, it's important to provide an arena of *acceptance, understanding, nonjudgment,* and *active listening* to the students. My personal goal is to be a "role model" for kindness where students can feel safe and comfortable to ask questions and be responded to in a way that shows interest. I do this modeling so it will be emulated, and I hope it is. Patients in the hospital want to be attended to in an emotional way, or so I have discovered. So, my behavior with students must match what is important for the patients to receive.

As a nurse educator and a human being, I strongly think that kindness comes under the umbrella of compassion and empathy. This is demonstrated in the article "A Patient's Story," written by Kenneth Schwartz for *The Boston Globe Magazine* in July 1995. In this article, Schwartz emphasized that compassion can be shown by acts of kindness whether it be through physical touch, a smile, a consoling word(s), or personal sharing of experiences. He claims this assisted him in coping with his sudden diagnosis of terminal cancer (Schwartz, 1995).

As a professor at a university, I taught an undergraduate psychology nursing theory course that required an "Intensive Writing Assignment." This required the students to write a research paper that required two drafts and then the final paper. Each paper had to be reviewed by the professor with provisions for constructive feedback on the written work. This meant grammar and content were evaluated. The article I chose for the students to critique was "A Patient's Story" by Kenneth Schwartz. Upon reading the article, the students were usually impressed by the powerful story, because of the patient's struggle during his advancing illness to maintain his positivity, strength, and courage both for himself and his family. From the compassionate care of the hospital staff involved in his care from the nurse, radiation therapist, the anesthesiologist to his physician, the patient felt a soothing comfort and a sense of safety.

That trait of *kindness* was exhibited by one of my nursing students in my Psych Theory class. Upon writing the first draft for the "Intensive Writing Assignment," he chose to include a personal example, as he felt it strongly related to the experience Schwartz gave in his writing. The nursing student was on a medical-surgical unit for his clinical rotation when a patient was refusing to get out of bed. The staff became increasingly irritated and angry with the patient to the point of nagging the patient because of his utmost resistance and non- adherence to the regimen. The nurses were apparently aware and concerned that reduced mobility could lead to decreased circulation. This would affect the physical care of the patient, but their method of communication proved to be a block in motivating this person.

The nursing student realized that therapeutic communication, compassion, and empathy taught to him as a student were not being used by the staff. This apparently led to the increased negative behavior of the patient. The student decided to sit down and spend time talking with the patient and discovered that the patient was depressed over a severe and recent stressor. After their discussion, the patient felt heard, listened to, and understood. Realizing the kindness and compassionate care of the nursing student, exhibited by his taking time to listen to him, the patient agreed to get out of bed.

In addition, in my opinion, the student provided an atmosphere of acceptance and of being nonjudgmental which exhibited his usage of kindness. This, to me, represented a fine example of how kindness in the form of compassion and empathy, which are incorporated in therapeutic communication, can improve both the patient's physical and mental well-being by enhancing a patient's feeling of safety and comfort.

Summary Camp

By Jake Levy

Fairness: Over the summer I worked at a sleep away camp. Campers came for seven weeks to build bonds with others, participate in different activities, and grow as people. There's no technology allowed so campers must rely on old school forms of communication. This form of communication is simply talking with one another. A give and take and back and forth is what's evidenced. Even with that the new environment for a lot of first-time campers brings homesickness. It can be scary to be away from the place one is used to being.

I have found that there are a lot of strategies to attempt to quell this homesickness feeling in campers but there is one strategy which seems to do the trick. It's based around the child's idea of fairness. What we do first as camp leaders is listen to each child share how they're feeling and why they feel that way. Also, in this sharing there is talk about what their experience has been so far up to that point of camp. What I have experienced, oftentimes, is the negative response. As leaders we listen to the sharing and try to also remind campers to talk about the positive. Going with the idea that fairness is getting what you need, we talk about needing to have a good time at camp. So, we emphasize the positive aspects of camp. For example, we ask what was something enjoyed.

We ask campers to describe a glass half filled with air and half filled with water. We share that there are two ways to describe the glass, both are equally right. The glass can be half full of water or it can be half empty. To be fair doesn't always apply to rules but to perspectives as well. It doesn't matter which way the camper describes the water as you share with them both perspectives.

So, when it comes to being homesick the camper usually wants to go home as the answer, but did they give camp a fair chance? There are good and bad parts, but if they only see camp as bad and never see their glass half full, they are never being fair to camp or themselves. Being in the middle of nowhere means that your parents can't come and get you at the drop of a hat. So, the campers might as well give it a fair shot by approaching camp from the other perspective—the positive one.

Kids may not be able to understand the concept of a different perspective, but they understand the idea of fairness, even if they struggle with it. Fortunately, in most cases after this conversating with homesick campers they go on to loving camp and do not return to a homesick state. We know this by simply going up to these kids and asking what their cup of water looks like, and they say, "Half full," as we're told something good that the camper experienced. So, the camper has related something positive and realized that what's needed is a good feeling about camp. Telling us things that make them happy deters from the negative and emphasizes the cup half full, as well as a positive attitude—looking for and finding what's liked about camp is the result. But there is also realizing that what is needed is a positive perspective and that's what's ultimately shared.

What's That Sound?

By M. Schiering

Good Citizen: The fifth-grade schoolteacher, Peggy, was driving home from school on a hot very late spring day. As she traveled along the Parkway, the sun beat down endlessly, when suddenly, added to the traffic and miserably steamy weather with the car's air conditioner broken, there was a "cathode" sound. Thinking that the car beside her had a flat tire, she sped up to avoid having any problems. However, all the increased speed did was cause the sound to come faster. Ah, the flat tire was on Peggy's car! What to do? What to do?

Within the next few moments, Peggy ascertained that it was best if she pulled off the road and handled the situation. There was a little inlet to make this transition relatively easy. And so, she proceeded to park the car, put her head against the headrest, sigh, and then get out of the vehicle to "check things out." She walked around the car starting with a look-see at the driver's side tire. It was fully inflated and so was the passenger's side tire. A quick glance showed the tire behind that one to be completely flat with the rim touching the ground. What to do was easy. She sat down, cross-legged, in front of the tire, stared at it, and cried.

Cars sped by with no acknowledgement of her car barely inside the inlet. She buried her head in her arms trying to think of a way out of this dilemma. There was no solution in sight, as she sat there waiting for . . . who knows what? Perhaps help.

After what seemed like an hour, but was only twenty minutes, she felt a "presence" by her side. Looking to her right, she was surprised to see a pair of dirty sneakers worn by a man around fifty years of age. He had grease-stained shorts and a T-shirt. Also his two front teeth missing. He smiled at her, and that's how she saw his teeth were not there. She felt a small gasp escape her lips as the man said, "You seem to have a flat tire." She thought, "He has stated the obvious." His first comment was immediately followed by, "Do you know how to change the tire?" In fact, she did not know how to do that and shook her head to indicate her not knowing. "Well, then let's get to the trunk of your car and let me change the tire for you."

Hesitatingly, she got up and moved to the car's trunk. She phoned her husband to let him know what was happening. Next, she told this good citizen that the trunk was full of stuff. This meant students' large board projects going home for the semester. The man, Gary, related that it probably wasn't too bad, but she knew it was.

Opening the trunk to get the spare tire, lug wrench, and jack, the man who she now knew was named, Gary, physically took several steps backward when the trunk popped up and he saw what was inside. "Loaded with stuff? What is all this? The things I need are buried under these tri-fold boards. We'll have to move them to the back seat." Peggy explained that this area too was filled, and they'd have to lay the contents of the car's trunk on the ground or lean these against a nearby tree.

So, the next half an hour found these two strangers to one another unloading the trunk, getting the needed tire-changing equipment, and Gary's setting to work on changing the flat. This took a little while, maybe another half an hour. Then, there was putting the damaged tire in the trunk and all the things leaning against trees or on the ground placed back where they'd been.

Slapping his hands together, Gary said, "Mission accomplished!" Peggy asked what made him stop to help her. He responded, "That's easy. My mom told me if you ever see someone in distress, help that person. You were in distress, for sure!" Peggy thanked Gary and realized she only had two dollars and how much this whole thing would have cost if she'd had to call a car service person. She offered him a check, but he refused it. He said that wasn't necessary.

Peggy then asked him his favorite charity, and, with his reply, she took out a check and made it out to cash for him to give to that organization. Gary smiled and said, "Thank you." Peggy smiled and said, "It's I who thank you and your mom for her words of wisdom to you when you were younger. I appreciate your stopping. I've a long ride home, but now I can accomplish that and be safe at the same time. Truly, you are a good citizen. Thank you, a thousand times. I'll pay this thoughtfulness forward in your name."

Gary and Peggy shook hands and then parted with Gary's driving back onto the highway and a short time later, Peggy's, doing the same. "What a day" she thought. "I believed that there was no way out of that horrible mess, and then someone came along and helped me. An act of generosity and kindnesses—a good citizen! Who'd have figured that?"

Types of Kindness

By Amy Meyers

Kindness: Some people are generally kind human beings and others may be kind but don't necessarily wear it on their sleeves. They don't mention or show off their kindness. My story is about someone who was generally a kind person. There was more than one person. But first, let me explain something about myself. I'm not someone who asks for help or even accepts it mostly when it's offered. Perhaps that is why I am quite impacted when someone does something that acknowledges me. Well, this may be a different type of acknowledgment: I'm not talking about flowers or jewelry or even a card. Let me explain.

In my home growing up, I did not have a voice. I had an overwhelming sibling who was seemingly quite confident, articulate, and well informed. I felt I paled in comparison. And this was either by my own sense of self, or through the parental collusion of honoring my sibling's forthrightness of opinion and experiences. For the most part, I remember sitting at many family dinners quite silent. My voice was not solicited or engaged. For me it's important to note that both explicitly and implicitly my voice was squandered or wasted.

Now, as an adult I have fully found and use my voice. After much vulnerability and risk-taking I allowed myself to be heard. And yet, occasionally, the old me, the child me rears her ugly head and I hesitate to share my thoughts or experiences, especially in group settings.

Well, let mention here that I belong to a book club. And I have been a member of this great group of women for approximately six years. They all have children close in age, and I am the only childless member. When they talk about their parenting issues, I participate and offer my input. I feel like an equal. Though mostly I listen and offer some humor. I don't like to take up a lot of space.

This past week, I had a loss in my family. I was moved by it, partially due to its suddenness. And there was anxiety, as I was named the legal guardian of her ten-year-old child. I love this child with a fierceness reserved for one's own child, and yet the idea of being a parent at my age was something I had not imagined. Still, I love and adore this child.

So, you may wonder, what is the connection to kindness? I felt the need to process my feelings and stepped out of character and presented my experience to my book club friends. As I did, in walked another member of the group who was exasperated by her child's flu-like illness as he was away at college. She was very worried. The group immediately tended to her. I felt dropped. I felt neglected. And I was embarrassed by my own feelings. I felt ashamed at being an adult and feeling this need for attentiveness. I felt a rekindled from childhood. A sense of emotional abandonment.

I waited patiently to see if anyone would circle back to me. It didn't happen. But after moving on to a couple of other topics, one group member turned to me and said, "Well let's get back to Amy." This held the group accountable. This was an act of kindness to draw the attention back to me. I also found this book club member to be empathic and endearing. From my perspective, it was exactly what I needed and hadn't been able to bring myself to do for myself.

From this point forward, the group engaged in my issue with attentiveness, advice, and an openness that restored my desire to use my own voice more often; advocate for myself. This kindness renewed my belief in humanity.

While this may not be a story that one generally thinks of in regard to an act of kindness, those around me were active listeners and with that exhibition of being interested in me, I witnessed a personal caring gesture . . . a kind act of listening and sharing. I think that most of us just want to be heard and understood. And many people, well meaning, don't know how to offer that exchange of thoughts and feelings when someone shares a deep feeling.

Often, when listening to a story, we think about what we are going to say next; we may silver-line it with "Oh it's going to get better" or "At least you have such and such." We may actually interrupt the one sharing and offer a similar experience. What I believe most people really need is for others to be able to sit with their feelings, to be with them at the moment, and to convey they "get it." But we tend to mistake showing how we get it with other modes of communication, such as mentioned earlier.

Holding someone, truly emotionally holding someone is being able to sit with the discomfort of the feelings they are expressing. And THAT is something that sounds easy but oftentimes may not be easy to provide. It holds more weight than it may feel to the person offering it, because we tend to want to problem-solve and make others feel better. Again, we are well meaning! When someone is in distress or feeling dismayed, a true act of kindness is being there by holding the person in distress, actively listening to that person, or just being attentive to what is being shared. Should you ever be in such a situation, I invite you to try one of these modes of kindness!

Where's the Money?

By G. Schiering

Trustworthy, Dependable, and Responsible: It was a rather cold winter's day when the man went to the grocery store to buy a few items for the evening meal. A short drive from the house, maybe ten to fifteen minutes at most, was not a big hassle. Parking the car was a completely different matter, as the lot was full of cars. Still, he found a space and went to do the shopping.

Traveling up and down isles and getting the food he recognized the next-door neighbor shopping too. He went over, and they struck up a conversation that lasted longer than it did to get to the store in the first place. Nonetheless, they then continued selecting groceries. It was about 5:00 p.m. when the man realized he only needed one more item to complete the shopping list and then go home and making the meal for the family would be done. He was feeling a bit pressured because he knew dinner would be a little late unless there was a quick checkout station.

As he looked for the twenty items or less sign to be lit, he saw it wasn't. So, he joined the five-person long line, which was a nuisance. The store music didn't help his impatience, nor the two ladies in front of him having a detailed conversation about their dogs. But he waited rather patiently, and soon enough it was his turn to put the groceries on the counter and have them rung-up and bagged. Well, he'd be doing the bagging with the bags he'd brought from home.

With groceries rung up, he reached for the money in his back pocket and came up with nothing but air. "Where was the money?" he thought. He wondered, "Did I leave it at home? Did someone take it from my pocket?" Just as he told the grocery clerk that he must have left his money at home, the person behind him in the line said "I think you dropped this when you reached into your back pocket. I found this group of twenty-dollar bills on the floor. And since I know I don't have any cash on me and you seem to be looking for it, I figure this is yours."

The man looked quizzically at this person, and, thanking her, he then put out his hand to take the cash. "Hmmm," he thought, "Did this person just give me this money seeing I didn't have any or did it really drop out of my pocket when I reached for it? I'm not sure I'll ever know."

The man thanked the woman for paying attention and seeing him drop the money or see it fell out of his pocket. He explained that he was in a bit of a rush and how he had thought the money for the groceries was there, but her finding it was definitely a huge help. He said, "You are very kind to have given me this money, as you could have easily used it for your own groceries. You're very kind and thank you." The woman nodded and said, "You're welcome."

The man went out of the store and put the groceries in the car and drove home. He told his family what had happened, and all the kids were surprised. Even his wife seemed a bit shocked. But she said, "Trustworthy people are all around, and it just takes an act of kindness to realize this." The man agreed and went about making dinner and enjoying the evening with his family's praising his cooking.

Chapter 16

Short Stories

INTRODUCTION

The short stories in this chapter are for use during reading lessons, creative writing times, or independent writing for classroom sharing and community building. They may also serve as an impetus for students' creative or informative writing. The pages of this chapter are filled with stories written by students at Yavapai College's Osher Lifelong Learning Institute (OLLI), located in Prescott, Arizona. There are also contributions from some of this author's friends and family members, and other people met along this author's life's path. The main thing, regardless of who wrote the stories, is that they are here for your use in a classroom as part of a lesson plan. The first story in this chapter is for use during instruction time. What story you choose will depend on the strategy you're using and how well it applies to the topic of your lesson.

Then again, you may want simply to enjoy the story and use it for classroom sharing when inviting students to write their own stories. Of course, using this chapter to its fullest potential, when having such an assignment in your classroom, invites the students to tell their stories. The emphasis in the previous sentence is "tell," as opposed to reading their stories. This way, the class can practice the guidelines of an oral presentation as seen in chapter 7 of this book. Or, for SEL, they are sharing their perspectives on a topic which can be used for classroom discussion and application of thinking skills. Read on, dear readers, and enjoy the life experiences of others.

You're invited to determine if you could ever be in such a situation and, if so, imagine your reaction. Take time to identify story characters, their personality, the moods of the story, the setting (time and place) events, and the story problem and solution if there is one. There's much to be said for writing and storytelling, as it brings the reader into a reflective and communitive realm and then, at a future date, adds to one's memories if these were emotionally significant.

Author's Note: At each story's end there is an activity that may be done to emphasize that particular story's events, and other story elements.

Digging for a Fossil: A Bullying Story

By Marjorie S. Schiering (2001)

It was the students' third-grade class where for the past week the study of fossils was the topic of the science unit. Fossils were explained to be the remains or traces of plants, insects, or animals that lived a very long time ago. It could be something as simple as a leaf print on a rock, a skeleton from eons past, or something that had been trapped in the soil or ice. They were from prehistoric times. The class had discovered this definition using Google search and, of course, the teacher-provided information.

The class lessons involved a slideshow, work on the Smart Board, and some hands-on activities. One of those was to make an animal that existed long ago. These were buried in a very large plastic dirt-filled box the teacher had provided. Everyone was told that these would be "discovered" at the end of the school year when the students would dig in it for their fossils, and see what they retrieved—their own or someone else's. Either way, they were to identify the fossil and put it on display on the corner bookshelf. It had been a "fun" set of lessons in which everyone was involved. Hmm, what did the teacher call it—not involved, but "actively engaged."

This story begins a week after the making and putting of the pretend fossils in the container. The student, Sal, got to thinking, "What if I go digging in the schoolyard and find a fossil? Could there be one there? How deep would I have to dig? Well, why not give it a try?" With all this focused thinking, Sal decided to do this on Thursday afternoon.

Bringing a large spoon to school in her lunch box, she waited until after her class ended at 3:00 p.m. Fossil digging time had arrived!. Projecting her thoughts to finding a fossil, she decided that, when she discovered one, she'd bring it home. She'd have her mom wash it off, find a place to sell it, perhaps on E-bay, and then the family would become millionaires. This thinking, shall we say, was "imaginative" at the very least. But, to her credit, she was known for her creativity, out-of-the-box thinking, and making up stories to bring a smile to others. And, sometimes, she would invent things. The thought of being a millionaire was "cool." Some would look at this and say that this third grader was stupid, but she thought, "Let them think what they want."

Thursday was a pleasant temperature day. She selected a spot not far from the baseball diamond. Spoon in hand, she began her search, carefully making a mound of dirt to the right of where she sat cross-legged on the ground. Not too far along in her venture, four of her classmates appeared in front of her. Billy, Angela, Marilyn, and Rog called her name, and she looked up at them. "EWWW," said Marilyn, "you're disgusting. Look at you!" the others countered, "You're a mess, gross, ugly, ugh!"

"What was going on here?" she wondered, as she asked them what they meant. They readily explained as their faces scrunched up and they yelled at her, "You have Cooties, the invisible bugs are crawling all over your skin. They're in your hair and everywhere."

She began to cry and asked in her sobbing voice, "If they are invisible, how can you see them?" "Because we can. You're so stupid, digging for fossils and now the bugs are all over you. Don't come near us, don't touch us, or they'll spread."

Sal jumped up and threw her spoon down on the ground. As her classmates kept taunting her, she ran home and pleased that they didn't follow her, she nonetheless cried the four blocks to her house. Coming through the door and audibly crying, Sal's mother asked what was happening. She ran upstairs, commanding her mom to leave her alone. "But you're upset, what's happening?"

Sal responded between sobs, "Nothing, leave me alone. Leave me alone." Her mom, concerned for her daughter, said she was coming up the stairs. "NOOOOO" was Sal's reply. "Don't do that, don't do that. I will be fine." Her mom yelled back, "But you're crying so hard."

Through her tears she yelled, "I'll be okay, just leave me alone!" And so, the mother did.

Fifteen minutes went by, and the child was rubbing her eyes, still crying, and trying to find the Cooties. "Maybe, I'll be able to see them if I rub my skin hard enough," she thought. Dad arrived home and spoke to her mom. He appeared at the bottom of the stairs below the landing. After it, there were five more steps. He yelled up to, Sal, and asked her what was happening. "What's the matter?" Still crying she screamed back at him that nothing was wrong, and he should stay away from her. The tone in his voice was commanding, as commanding as his words for her to come downstairs and let him see her. Her response was just as vocal, and there was a resounding, "No!"

Again, her dad told her to come downstairs, but this time he used her first and middle name. She knew this meant she was in trouble and followed his command. Slowly, she went down the stairs. "Don't touch me," she pleaded. Her dad asked, "Why not?" Overcome with so much happening since digging for fossils, she responded, "I don't have a Coot, I have lots of them . . . Cooties! Billy, Angela, Marilyn, and Roger told me. They're all over me!"

Calmly, her dad asked her to let him have a look. She yelled, "They are invisible!!! But these kids saw them." Her dad again asked her to please let him have a look at her spreading out her arms to either side of her body. She complied, still crying, but more softly now. He looked at her arms and said he sees nothing. "That's because they're invisible!" she responded. Her dad instructed her to take off her shoes and socks and spread her toes apart because this is a common hiding place for these Cootie bugs. She complied as he announced again that she had none. "But they're invisible!" she screamed and then calmly changed her tone as she lowered her voice. "Daddy, they are invisible."

Her father reached into his right pants pocket and pulled out his wallet. Then, he removed a card and showed it to her. Not much of a reader she saw the words "New York State" across the top of the card. This card he held was his NYS driver's license, but he explained it differently and slowly said, "This is my Official Cootie Inspector Card for our state." Sal looked at him quizzically and asked what that means. He responded with, "It means the Cooties aren't invisible to me, because I have been approved to check for them. I can see them if they are there. I have a special Cootie sight ability. They're not invisible to me." He showed how the card had his address and says New York State and then how the other lines have his birthdate and the small print, which she couldn't read, and he said it read, "Official Cootie Inspector."

"Really, you're an inspector? How come you never told me?" He responded with, "Well, there never was a need until now. Tell me what's happening because you definitely do not have Cooties." Sal explained all that happened at the schoolyard near the baseball field. Her dad smiles and told her that it'd be great to discover a fossil and become millionaires and he admired her venturing forth to start the "dig-of-discovery." He stated strongly that it was not nice of her classmates to bully her by saying she had Cooties and that they were, perhaps, jealous of her fossil dig and wanted to get her away from it so they could dig. "Hmmm," she thought, "That made sense."

Her dad then told her that perhaps these four classmates had Cooties. "Listen carefully, here's what you must do. Go to school tomorrow and tell those kids that your dad is an Official Cootie Inspector and he's coming to their house to inspect them because they might be the ones with this invisible bug."

The next day, Sal did exactly that. The four kids were waiting for her outside the school's main entrance. They were surrounded by other kids who were all chanting, "Don't come near us, you can't go to school. You have Cooties. She yelled, "Stop it! I do not have Cooties! My dad is an Official NYS Cootie Inspector. He looked me over and said I am Cootie free. He said he's coming to your houses because you're probably the ones with Cooties. Leave me alone!"

There was a gasp from all the kids. They wondered, "Could this be true? Best not to take a chance." They simultaneously thought of inviting Sal into their group as they all walked into school together and went to their classroom to start the day. Never again was there such an incident with anyone on the Cootie topic. Sal thought, "I've been saved! Maybe they were bullying me or wanted to use my 'dig site' like Dad said. Or maybe they were afraid that my dad, the Official Cootie Inspector, was real and he would come to their house and see they had Cooties."

Because of the cleverness of her dad and due to his being a protector of his daughter, the incident passed. And although it is remembered, it faded, as most bullies do over time. The school kids didn't bother her again, and she was left alone but was asked to join in events and be part of a group that had as its motto, "No bullying anyone . . . ever!" She joined the group.

Activity for this story: Form a classroom Bully-free Zone. Meeting in groups create a poster announcing this idea and the rules that apply for having a safe classroom. Or, try the next idea.

Another Activity for This Story

1. First, in science, address the topic of what makes something a fossil. Then create a list of ten to fifteen fossils that exist now. Pose the question of what might be a fossil 1,000 years from now. This brings the class into a discussion that calls for reflection, probably some research, and a good deal of comparing with thought projection. This is an at-home or at-school activity depending on the availability of soil or sand. Obtain a large box and fill it one-fourth with the earth or sand substance.
2. Working together as a whole class have the students make a list of things that are common to us now, but they think might be fossils a 1,000 years from now. Some things may be shoes, computers, cell phones, types of housing, schools, history of a country, types of food, marketplaces, etc. Have the students make a list of ten to fifteen of these for classroom sharing.
3. Working with playdough, clay, or some other substance that can be formed or molded create miniatures of these listed items. These are the representations of fossils and they each need to be labeled.
4. Get a large box or plastic container and fill it with soil or sand. Put the labeled objects in different parts of the box for a future fossil dig.
5. At different times during the next months of school have this box as an activity for a fossil dig. The students will then have the opportunity to write about their experience of digging for fossils and increase their scientific knowledge on this topic, as well as observe what is of value today and may not be in centuries to come. The Why of this is another lesson extension. Why do things become extinct or of lesser value as time passes? The thinking skill of speculation is emphasized.
6. Further use of this activity is to determine why what we call fossils now came to be that.

The Helmet: A Time Travel Tale

By Jerry Thurber

Grandma had a dark, musty-smelling basement. Off to one side was an old Wringer Washer Machine with rollers you hand-cranked to squeeze the water out of the clothes. Granny still used it. Also, a pool table was in the middle of the room just below the only light bulb in the basement. You had to lean over the table to pull the chain. The light barely pushed back the corners of darkness. It smelled like cigarettes, wet clothes, and forgotten dreams.

In one corner of the room, someone, long ago, had built a small storage room by building two walls into the corner abutting the basement's foundation. The walls had windows caked with the dust of decades. My brother Jack and I used to love running down to the basement. It felt like an adventure. We explored all over it but didn't go into that storage room. It felt creepy.

The one light in the basement failed to penetrate those dusty windows. Items on the shelves remained shrouded and obscure. But we grew older and more daring. When Jack was twelve and I was nine, Jack dared me to go into the room. Jack was always daring me to do things like the time he dared me to see how high up the stairs at our house I could jump from. The game was over when I broke my ankle. The consequence only slowed him down until I was healed. It was hard to say "No" to Jack.

I walked over to the door, turned the knob, and slowly pushed the door open. The hinges were so old and disused they didn't squeak but made a grinding noise as the indurated rust broke loose. The room was full of cobwebs and dust. But the shelves held a treasure of stories waiting to be retold. Who was that lady in the framed painting leaning against the self, what was in the dull black box, who had used that chipped teacup, and why is that word in an old leather scabbard hanging on the wall behind a pile of boxes?

When my brother saw that no monsters or ghosts were attacking me, he bravely joined me in my search. Back in one corner of the room, up on a high shelf, we could see an old army helmet. Covered in dust and cobwebs, I reached up and pulled it down. Jack yanked it from my hands: "Let me see that," he said; then quickly dropped it when a huge spider crawled out of it. I picked it up and wiped it off with an old rag. No more spiders but I did find two holes in it. One hole was in the front of the helmet, about three inches above the right eye and off to the side; it was just big enough for my finger to fit through. The other hole was exactly opposite it in the back.

"I bet that is a bullet hole," said Jack. "Cool, put it on." I think Jack was worried there were still spiders in it and so was I, but I lifted the helmet to my head and put it on it. Suddenly, I was in a trench with dozens of other men.

Some were bleeding, and some were slumped against the sides of the walls. They all wore dirt-encrusted brown wool uniforms, held rifles with bayonets attached, and helmets that looked just like the one I had on.

A man approached me, a Sergeant, I think. I watched a lot of war movies and knew most of the insignia. He said, "I know what you are thinking, Lieutenant, Don't do it. We all hear that horse suffering, but if you try and go over that wall, you get killed." I yanked the helmet off my head. Jack grabbed it from me and put it on. I yelled at him to stop, but I was too late. He started goofing off pretending he was some army guy. Then he took the helmet off.

"Did you see it?" I asked him.

He responded, "See what?"

I shot him a quizzical look and said, "The trench, the men in uniforms with guns, did you talk to the sergeant?" He quickly responded with,

"What are you talking about?"

I patiently explained to Jack that, when I put on the helmet, I was suddenly in a war. He looked upward and gave an exasperated sigh before saying, "Yeah sure, you must have been hallucinating or something. Let's look around some more." I didn't push it any further, I began to question myself as well and decided I should just let it be. Jack and I looked around the room some more, got bored, and went out and played pool until Grandma (we called her Granny Annie) called down to tell us it was time to wash up for dinner.

Sitting at the table, I asked my grandpa about the helmet, and he explained, "Oh yeah, that old thing. It belonged to my dad. He was a veterinarian in World War I. He took care of the horses."

"How did it get a hole in it?" I asked.

"Well," he said, "Your great grandfather was in a particularly bloody battle and one of the horses got shot in the rear leg. Horses were used to carry supplies or ferry the wounded back to the trenches. The horse went down and started screaming something terrible. Your great-granddaddy couldn't take it. A sergeant had told him not to go, but he was a Lieutenant and didn't have to listen to him, and so he climbed up the ladder and crawled to the horse. The wound wasn't bad, but it must have hurt the horse terribly. He was able to give it a painkiller that allowed him to sneak the horse back to safety, but as he was running back with the horse, a bullet hit his helmet and passed clear through. It missed him completely. All the troops started calling him "lucky" after that. And I guess he was, as he made it back and ended up living to age 83."

I tried that helmet on several times over the years but never saw the image again, and I've always wondered what that was about. A touch of science fiction or time travel?

Activity for this story: Using pictures of horses or animals from the internet, print, or have students try to draw these. Have them be five by six or eight in height and length. Next, color the pictures if they are drawn ones. Cut out each horse or animal picture and make a border for a section of the classroom wall or hallway. This is done by taping the animal pictures together. Title the section, *Animal Short Stories*, and have the students, working in partnerships, alone or in small groups, write an imaginative story about an animal. Then, have them paste or tape the stories to the wall inside the border. This bordered section is then a place in the classroom to read one another's creative writing. Change the border or topic throughout the school months or semester. Invite other classes into the room or hallway for "wall reading."

The Choice

By Jolie Schiering

We all have that one friend, well most of us have that ONE friend! You know, that friend who was with you through thick and thin. The one that changed groups/interests with you, as you got older. That soul sister/brother that you could always share anything with and you were always just "SOLID," no matter what it was.

Now I understand not everyone has that one friend forever. We all change as we advance in age and climb up the ladder of life, but we all know someone like this or have known someone like this in our lives at some point. This story is about ONE person involving betrayal, forgiveness, understanding, kindness, and CHOICE.

I had been friends with my "sister from another mister" a.k.a. "my soul sister" for over fifteen years. Going from community college to university, post-grad work, full-time entering the job force, and then on to personal life advancements (marriage, kids, and death of loved ones), we were on our course together. I had a solid friend group (but there is always that "one bestie" in the group). I had that for close to fifteen years, and then, it happened . . .

The ultimate betrayal came when I shared a personal secret with her. Three months later, at my 34th birthday party, I learned that the secret was shared with "my whole friend group" and EVERYONE KNEW something I didn't want anyone in the world to know. At the time, it was one of the biggest secrets I had. I was mortified at my own birthday party, in my own house. She was not present for other reasons. I found myself speechless. Having to confront my own personal demons at my own party, in my own house, was unreal to me. A secret I shared only with her. I could not deny anything and was forced to take ownership of my actions, which were not the best. This was the ultimate betrayal. How could someone do that to me, let alone my trusted confidant!!!!!

When confronted after the event, she brushed it off. Then, of course, we spoke harsh words to each other. So, what does one do? I could forgive and move on, as if it were no big deal, or I could fight back, blab a personal secret of hers. I personally could not even fathom the latter. It was a harsh break-up or divorce. At least that's what my therapist said.

Yes, I had to go into therapy for two years at the loss of this friendship. I had never had a relationship that had lasted so long (almost two decades). A solid kinship between us two, and one slip of the tongue and a secret would end our friendship. Fifteen years of my life and a person I held so dear to my heart and my family's heart was gone! It was the death of a lifelong trust and friendship with my "soul sister sibling."

I completely changed my life group; I started hanging out with new people and leaving my past poor choice behind. Life went on for me as it did for her. We were out of touch for many years. I forced myself to forget her number and our stories together. I tried to move on with my life, knowing it had a little less sparkle, forever changing my relationships with people even to this day. I encouraged myself to remember the small spats and bad traits she had and move past that friendship. As I stated it was like a death to me. Some may say a growing-up moment. My dad said, "They are tender hurts, the hurts that pull at your heartstrings."

I was in North Carolina for a cousin's wedding a few years later. Life was going well for me. I started a new business, I ran a marathon, went skydiving, and traveled all over the United States. Then it happened! I started getting calls from random people whom I hadn't heard from in months or even years! All calling about this one person. The person who betrayed me left years ago, the one whom I spent over a year in therapy to get over, the person who changed my outlook on the human race.

I learned that life was unraveling for her. She was making horrible life choices. She was going through a divorce, facing the challenges of motherhood (teenagers, of course), and massive career failure along with substance abuse. She was reaching out in desperation to others and acting out in ways that would cause long-term damage to herself and others in her life.

Now I know a person's first thought might have been "You left this friendship years ago; you moved on with your life the best you could." However, my first real response was why? Why would all these people be reaching out to me? I was over the loss of the friendship. I was over a thousand miles away on a vacation, at a wedding, a time of celebration! Why would I be getting all these calls? I felt I was being pushed back into something I absolutely wanted nothing to do with, let alone a person I wanted nothing to do with anymore.

Then the final call came. and another long-time person told me, "It is you! Don't you get that? I think YOU are the only person who can pull her out of the nightmare she is in." These are desperate actions of a person in need. What choice are you going to make? Walk away and let this person go forever for a secret shared years ago that everyone already knew and let her continue her course of destruction and let life be and possibly end for her?"

Talk about a choice!!!!! What would you do? Well, I chose to write a letter and mailed it to the address I could never forget. I wrote about the wonderful human being she was, an excellent mother, and true friend (even though we had not spoken in years). I built her up and let her know she mattered to many more than she realized.

This letter might have been two or three pages long. Not once did I mention the betrayal or the hurt that I felt. I made no mention of the therapy I endured nor my major life accomplishments since her departure. I wrote a letter filled with all the love I felt for her and made sure she understood how much she meant to everyone, including me. I used powerful words to hopefully bring her back to her true self. I had no expectation of hearing a response, no attention I was seeking from this letter of love. Just my making **the choice** to give what I knew no other could give her. Giving her hope for a better tomorrow, kindness, and the confidence that she was going to make it through.

Months later, I ran into her older sister, and she stopped and thanked me for the letter I wrote to her baby sister. As tears poured down her face she told me what an amazing and impactful letter I'd written and how it changed not only her sister's life but hers too.

Again, months later, I was at a karaoke contest filled with all my friends from the past (the ones who knew I was no longer friends with this person), and in the middle of the fun festivities with my back to the door, all the music stopped (like in a movie), and it was silent while everyone stared at ME!

At first, I thought a mechanical error of the DJ had occurred. Then, like in a movie, she walked in the door and was now standing just behind me. Again, I had the choice to ignore or to embrace this person with a much-needed hug to put all the broken pieces of our lives back together. One more time a choice was made, and it was one of the best embraces I have ever had to this day.

That, my friend, is **the choice**! *One of forgiveness or holding onto a grudge.* Which one will you choose when it is your time to choose? Remember that the meaning of life is to find your gift and give it away to others. My friend and I are still good friends to this day. Again, I ask what choice will you make? *"The meaning of life is to find your gift; The purpose of life is to share it with others" (Pablo Picasso).*

Activity for this story: Passing notes, texting, or sending an email are three possibilities for this activity. If it's the latter two, then be sure that each person in the class texts to only one person they know waits for a response, and then texts another one or two persons if so chosen. The text/email is to say something that is right with the person being written to. Some sentences of positivity are the goal. And if there are no cell phones or classroom computers for this, then do a note pass in the classroom. This activity in that format is limited to saying something nice about a class member. Of course, the title of the note is, *Positive Message*. Whatever mode of communication is chosen, the idea is to get a response from that person and then ask that person to text, email, or send a note to someone else. Correspondence can go to friends, family members, teachers (present or past), or relatives other than immediate family. Call the activity, "Spread the Word of Positivity!" If so desired by participants, share the message sent and received. Do this activity several times a month.

"Driving the Truth Home"

By M. S. Schiering (2002)

It was a relatively warm day in the upstate town of Rochester, NY. Maggie had some friends who did the usual teenage things of the 1970s, not that these things were good ideas, but practiced behaviors nonetheless.

Author's Note: I strongly suggest that teenagers today not practice items one, three, and four.

These teenagers (1) tried cigarettes, (2) took driving lessons, (3) broke curfews now and again, (4) lied, (5) went to school sports events and concerts, and (6) enjoyed gathering at the local soda shop. But Maggie, this story's main character, was a bit different in that she was labeled a "goody-two-shoes." She would not get involved in the aforementioned numbers: 1, 3, and 4-antics. While she knew of her friends' escapades, she did not speak of them, maintaining their confidence in her. So, if they got in trouble, she'd be there for them, strictly as a good listener.

Her story takes place in Maggie's driveway on a very hot summer's day. Her dad had denied her driving lessons until she'd practiced going in and out of the driveway and turning the corner at the back edge of the house to do a "K" turn to go frontward out of the driveway. (The space for the "K" turn was a rather large rectangular portion of the driveway, between the house and the garage.) Then, in the street, she'd turn around and repeat going into the driveway, doing the "K" turn, and going out of the driveway. Simple? Not quite!

Sweating in the car, Maggie decided that this day would be the one of the hundred she'd thought about accomplishing that "K" turn to be the one to accomplish it. She trembled with fear, but was determined. Then, the strangest thing happened! Her brick house, as she was nearing the corner where the turn was to be made, jumped out into the driveway and she hit it!!!!!!!!!!!! Ugh!! "How could this happen?" She hit the house?! She got out of the car and examined the damage. With broken bricks all over the driveway, she saw only one solution. Use Elmer's Glue All to put the bricks back in place.

She got it, picked up the bricks, and meticulously glued them back where they belonged. She then went back in the house, took a plunger from the utility closet, and tried to plunge out the dent by the front right tire of the car. This accomplished, Maggie drove the car forward a little and made the right turn so the left side of the car was facing the garage. She carefully parked the vehicle. Thinking everything was okay, she went into the house and greeted her mom, joining her to watch television. Fast-forward: Dad came home stomping into the house yelling, "Who hit the house with the car???"

Maggie calmly said her mom was using the car earlier that day. Her mom denied this. Maggie asked why he thought the house was hit and the reply startled her. He said, "Well, it's pretty hot today, and whoever hit it used Elmer's Glue to put the bricks back in place, but the glue melted, so the bricks fell on the driveway. And then this person used a plunger to get the dent out of the car but forgot to put the plunger back in the house. So, that's on the driveway by the front fender. It's directly next to the area where the 'as yet not thoroughly removed dent' is located. Any response?"

Maggie explained that her girlfriend came over to borrow the car, and she knew she shouldn't have given permission, but her friend was desperate, and she hit the house when pulling forward to make the "K" turn. Dad's reply: "How much of that is a lie?" Maggie paused and said, "Uh, all of it." Red face flushing with remorse, she then said, "What happened is that strangely the corner of the house moved into the driveway, and I hit it. Dad smiled and replied: "The house moved into the driveway, or it stayed where it was, and you misjudged the distance between where you were driving to make the K turn?" Maggie replied, sheepishly, "Yeah, that'd be pretty much what happened. Sorry. I kind of lied to you about the house moving."

"Hmmm," Maggie's dad responded, "Had you told me the truth, that you hit the house because of misjudging the distance, then I'd have given you driving lessons and covered the cost of the repairs. Now, I will see to it that you get driving lessons, and I will pay for those. As for the car and house repairs, you'll need to take a portion of your salary at the shoe store and pay for them."

Author's Note: Maggie thought to herself, "It would have been best to stick to the truth the first time she said what happened! I think this has been a life-lesson for me, driving the truth home."

Activity for this Story: Have each class member make a list of three truths and three lies. Then, switch truths and lies with classmates and have them decide which is the truth and which is the lie. A good deal of discerning thinking is involved, and one can examine their own insight when making a decision.

The Howling Cat and Love

By Sue Nauman

One Saturday morning when living in Yavapai Hills, I was sitting at my desk working at the Computer when, WOOSH, up the trunk of the tree, right outside the window, there flew this black blur. I stood up but couldn't see the top of the tree. I looked down out the window, and there on the ground was a coyote looking menacingly up the tree.

I hurried to the front door and opened it, went out on the porch, and there at the tippy, tippy top of the tree was my very large, enormous, black cat, Isis. She was straddling two flimsy branches, which were swaying back and forth under her considerable weight. The coyote was gone. Isis, who never stops talking, so to speak, was muted by her fear. My other cat, a sleek athletic beauty, wanted out to see what was happening. So, we both just looked helplessly up at Isis.

After a few minutes, the big black, enormous Isis started howling. Have you ever heard a cat howl? It can be scary. Now she was swaying and howling non-stop. Not to be left out of the drama, my little athletic cat sat at the foot of the tree, growling, a protective sort of growl. This was designed to keep the coyote away. And they howled and they growled. Isis was, of course, too scared to move.

What to do? What to do? I went inside and decided against calling 911. So I looked up the Prescott Fire Department in the phone guide I had of emergency numbers. There was only one listing, even though a fire station's right around the corner from my house. I called the number I had, and a woman answered. The conversation when something like this:

Me: "Hi, I don't have a fire, but I do have a cat stuck in a tree and I need your help."
Woman: "We don't do cat rescues."
Me: "I've seen you do them all the time on television shows and in the movies."
Woman: "We don't do cat rescues."
Me: "But my cat's too high up and too scared to come down the tree."
Woman: "She'll come down when she's hungry. We don't do cat rescues."

Me: "She's so scared that she's howling. And the branch she's on might break."
Woman: "If she's still there next Saturday, we'll come and get her."

All through the phone call, I could hear the howling and growling in the background. So when I went back to the front porch, I was surprised to see that Isis was now on the roof of the house. I can't imagine how she managed that feat. Somehow, she'd leaped from the swaying branches to the roof. She wasn't even stuck in the right position for a leap. She wasn't any less scared or at least any less vociferous from the time when she was on the tree. The howling was non-stop! In the meantime, my other cat no longer sensed any clear and present danger and assumed her cat-like not caring, as she bedded down on the ground.

Again, what to do? I decided I'd wait and somehow the cat would come down. I went back to work at the computer, but all I could hear was the howling of Isis. Finally, it occurred to me that I needed to figure out how to do the cat rescue myself. So, I went to the garage, pulled out the step ladder, and put it under the eaves of the garage the place where the roof line was lowest and the ground level was the highest.

Next, I opened up the ladder, and very clearly it said, on the bottom step, "Weight limit 200 lbs." Well, that was iffy, but I was willing to risk it. I climbed the ladder as high as I could and called the cat. She stopped howling and ran over to where I was on the top of the ladder, although this was at least eight feet short of my being able to reach her. Or to put it another way, a great distance considering her position on the roof for her to jump and have a landing place on my shoulders.

And then there was this 200-pound weight warning. That meant my weight plus the weight of this truly enormous cat really pushing the limits of this boundary. Since there was no way I could reach her, she would have to jump and leap onto my shoulders. Would she even do that? Isis may be a fat cat, but she's not a dumb cat. And she, like all cats, is not likely to take that leap full of risk and uncertainty.

There I am, considering my weight combined with that of Isis, and adding the sheer momentum of her landing on my shoulders. "We'll be knocked over for sure," I thought. I was feeling both foolish and determined. I kept talking to the cat, calming her, and then encouraging her to jump by patting my shoulders. And suddenly, she did it! She jumped and landed on my shoulders, and her claws firmly dug into my back. The ladder wobbled a little but steadied. I held onto the ladder.

Very slowly, we climbed down to the ground. Isis wouldn't let go of my shoulders. I got down on all fours. She wouldn't let go. So, I lay flat on the driveway. After her considerable deliberation and what seemed like an eternity of feeling those fierce claws entrenched in my back, Isis finally let go. A successful cat rescue! What happened was both of us trusting that this ladder-to-roof idea would work. Ah, we both had faith and hope with love.

Activity for this story: It's your turn to be very imaginative. Design an activity for this story that addresses the love shown by the cat's owner toward her pet. What are ways to show animals caring? Or, have a class discussion about students' opinions concerning pet ownership. If a pet is owned, then ask for funny stories that may have happened with a pet. Then again, a few sentences about kindness to animals may suffice.

Why Are They Laughing?

By Susan Gerhart

Finally, it was graduation day. The auditorium was filled with Oregon Public School attendees and puppy raisers. They were sharing their happiness at the Guide Dog Trainer's Union's soon-to-be completed. I wondered what each of my four classmates would say as we took on our roles as guide dog handlers. Also, the fundraisers acknowledge our work. Appreciation for these persons' raising 5,000 dollars for training guide dogs was formidable, and our appreciation for this was being recognized.

I had thought seriously about my short speech. Luckily, classmate and former actor, Bryan, went first with a whole routine about sadly leaving the comfort and meals we'd enjoyed together for two weeks. The audience was now prepared to hear the rest of us speak. Still, I was nervous even though I was the "senior" graduate by many decades. Also, I was prone to making mistakes and rather overeducated with respect to my constituents, as I had my doctorate degree.

Giving human imaging to my guide dog, Corky, is something I did frequently. I referred to him as my blonde boy who hadn't yet licked my hands nor agreed to limit sniffing while on the job. In fact, I nearly failed out of the program until I showed trainers how I would yank him away from sniffing particular trees. Guide dog management certainly has special survival challenges. A trainer would help me at home now and again to map my local routes and identify downtown's dangerous street crossings. My animal–human relationship was more serious than I had expected.

Reflecting on the graduation ceremony, I realized that any graduation speech had to be concise and relevant to the situation of graduating with my guide dog. My speech was simple, as I stated that I always wanted to be best at "living in the moment." My guide dog had brought me that experience. And I omitted my hallucination of flying like a kite the night we walked around in the dark. Corky followed the trainer with my hanging onto the leash for dear life and having no sight at all. Truthfully, being blind, I still have that flying feeling when our six feet are synchronized, and Corky is in charge of reaching the curb and stopping. Indeed, our training may have saved me from a spill at the corner near the parking lot north of Chase Bank. Here were a lot of foliage-shaded patches of ice that the proprietress of the bank failed to clear.

Ah, back to the moment on stage. After my short speech came a long saga by the very experienced puppy raiser who had split duties with a beginner training family where a math professor took puppy Corky to sleep through his calculus classes. So, the puppy-raiser finished, and the audience laughed. What was that all about? We hadn't said anything funny. Corky had been standing still between us. We were led off the stage to a round of applause. I was puzzled about this reaction of the audience through the remaining talks and demonstrations, as well as fund-raising pleas. Why they laughed at us, I just didn't know.

Finally, a staff person explained to me that Corky had been fixated on me, with his head upturned right toward my "in the moment" sharing. Then he arched his head left to listen attentively through the puppy raiser appeals. When finished speaking, he turned his head and directly looked into the audience. That's what made them laugh. His black eyes and dark fur now stood out on a white face with gray-tinged ears flopping as his head moved from speaker to speaker and then frontwards, staring at the audience.

Was he thinking "What's the big deal?" Was he waiting for the anticipated treat he'd get for his good behavior during the presentations? Anyway, we graduated students now could concentrate our worries on the early morning airport fly-outs to our homes. We had questions and some of these were: "Would the TSA give us extra patting down or would our dog not want to follow us through the X-ray machine? Once on the plane, could we bend our dogs into their seat space? Would the shuttle home be on time? Where do our dogs go to the bathroom at an airport?" While we didn't have the answers right there and then, we did discover the answers to them when we got to the airport.

In the meantime, once on the flight home, and many times since then, I thought back to the graduation event and recalled the audience's laughing. I'll never know if Corky's expressions when facing the audience, as well as me, and the other speaker, were what caused this graduation attendees' outburst of delight. However, as Corky and I walk our daily routines, I know I appreciate the dangers we face together and the wonders of being guided to where to go.

As my blindness is ever present, my dog is endearingly supportive. And each day I give her that graduating doggie treat she so enjoyed back then. I think too that it's okay for people to stare at me and I always thank them, although I can't see them, when they yell, "Beautiful Dog!" He certainly has made my life that way, as he leads me through each day.

Activity for this story: Using the story author's experience, make an appreciation list by recognizing the things you see each day. Then, using your other senses write how you have used these. Using your imagination, create an appreciation poem for each sense. Example follows:

> Appreciation Poem: Sight
> Today was rather special.
> It is because I saw.
> My dog ran up to me.
> He gave me licks and all.
>
> Then another thing happened.
> My garden flowers bloomed.
> They are so lovely and special.
> I put some in my room.

LuluBelle

By Gayla Putnam

I looked into the stern eyes of my middle school's principal, Mr. G. This was the third time this week that I had been in his office. He seemed annoyed by this fact, as he drummed his fingers on the desktop. The dialogue went something like this:

Mr. G: "Well, I'm waiting. Why are you here this time?"
Me: "The same reason I was here yesterday. Mrs. L. won't call me by my name."
   Mr. G. (With exasperation and a sense of ongoing annoyance) "Your name is LuluBelle. It's on your registration, and it's your given name."
Me: "I hate that name. My name is Lou."
   Mr. G. gave a long sigh, and a threatening look was sent directly to me. "You're an eleven-year-old juvenile delinquent," he said with exasperation.

I was not sure what being a juvenile delinquent meant, but I thought it sounded daring as I left his office and decided to skip class and head to the park.
   I climbed high into my favorite tree that extended above the bluebird's nest. She squawked testily at me. I could see the whole town from my vantage point. I laughed when I saw old Mr. Gerber. Every day he went to the

newspaper box. He looked around, then shook it hard. The door fell open, and he took a paper without paying. I wondered what else might happen that would be exciting this day.

Soon, I saw the cute blond secretary come out the bank's back door. My brother said she was really attractive. She leaned against the wall and lit a cigarette. Then, just like clockwork, out came the big elderly president. He leaned close to her. It looked like they were whispering. I wondered what it was about and thought, "Hmm, I better not tell anyone what I'm seeing."

Then, a long black sedan pulled into the parking lot. It was one of those fancy cars. I was on instant alert. A man in a suit with a briefcase got out. He looked around furtively and started walking toward the back of the ball diamonds. He was a stranger. I watched him go into the woods next to my second favorite climbing tree that I had stopped climbing when some goshawks; a large short-winged hawk resembling a large sparrow hawk, made a nest in it. They were downright unfriendly birds and had attacked me viciously. Anyway, I saw the man reach up and put a bag into the tree hollow. Then he jumped back. One of the goshawks flew down and clawed his head. He covered it with this briefcase, ran back to his car, and roared away.

"What was in that bag?" I wondered. "Could it be money?" I waited a while and then climbed down the tree. I hurried home double-quick. I wondered, "Where was my bike helmet?" I found it and put it on and ran back to the tree hollow. The goshawks went crazy, but I was protected by my helmet. I took the bag, I peeked inside. It was money, loads of hundred-dollar bills.

My mind raced. It was a fortune. I could buy a new bike and trash my pink one with the white daisy basket. I could buy my mother a new mixer she wanted. I might even buy something for my brothers and sisters if they were nice to me. I crept deeper into the woods and followed the railroad tracks back home. I went to my room and hid the bag under the bed. I lay down. I would be so rich and I would never have to go to school.

That night I was restless. Questions I asked myself included: "What if a thief came and took my money? Had I been careful? Had anyone seen me?" I didn't sleep at all and was happy to get up the next morning. My mother was reading the paper when I sat down for breakfast. She glanced up and questioned what had happened to my hair. I quickly explained that I'd cut it last night and gotten rid of those "curly braids" I hated, and so I just whacked them right off my head.

Mom ran her fingers through my ragged hair and said, "We'll have to go to the salon and see if they can fix it. You'll be the death of me. What's wrong with looking pretty?" I explained how I disliked all that "girlie" stuff. And I continued with how I wanted to be a detective or an explorer, or maybe a space captain. At that time in my life, these were not female gender roles. Now, it's different. Anyway, my mom sighed and turned back to the paper.

Then she said, "What is this town coming to? A murder right here down by the tracks. It happened yesterday."

I jumped up. The picture showed a black sedan with the briefcase man slumped over the wheel. I shivered. I had listened to old radio programs as a class assignment to see if we could learn as much from listening as from watching television. Anyway, this clearly was a gangsters' group member thing. I knew the term, "gangsters," to be a group of violent criminals.

I thought, "They'll find me. I am as good as dead." I spent a quick moment imagining my family weeping at my funeral and then flew into action. I waited impatiently for Mom to go to work. I grabbed my dreaded pink bike. I put three of my sister's dolls in the basket over the money bag. No gang of thieves would suspect a girl on a pink bike to have their money.

Johnny, our neighbor boy, was standing on his porch. "LuluBelle, where are you going with those dolls? I thought you hated them?" I replied with how I was throwing them in the river because they made me sick. "Can I come with you?" he asked. And I replied, "NO, it's a private funeral. Get lost!"

I rode as fast as I could to the river and stopped in the middle of the bridge. I had placed a large rock in the bag so it would sink fast. I looked around. No suspicious activity. I heaved the bag into the deep dirty water. It quickly fell out of sight. The wretched money was gone. I headed to school. I knew I would be revisiting the principal as I was late. But, my life of crime was over or, more correctly, hiding a crime was over, and then . . . I saw myself back at Mr. G's office. This was going to happen because someone was going to call me LuluBelle when I wanted to be called Lou.

Activity for this story: Using the Hierarchy and Reciprocal Thinking Chart create a grid showing the thinking skills used in this story and when they took place. Share this on a Smart Board with the class. Allow for comparison and contrast of perceived applications for a whole-class discussion on the identification of thinking skills and phases.

Another activity for this story: Using your own name, create an acronym poem to describe you. Example follows.

My name is Margie
And I like my name because it describes me:
Responsible is what I am.
Generous too.
Interesting to talk with, and
Energetic for sure!

What are the keywords in this poem that describe the person? Discuss in class what descriptive words were used for each person's poem. Then, write these words on the board for a word wall of adjectives.

Keeping the Basketball

By George Schiering

It wasn't many years ago when my wife and I were asked to join our son and his wife at a basketball game to be held in Madison Square Garden. The big attraction was that the seats were courtside! This meant they were in the second row. My wife was enamored with the idea and accepted the invite. We could hardly wait for the evening to arrive. Although we'd never been in this building, we knew of its amazing reputation.

When we got to the Garden, the outer lobby was a massive arrangement of different foods from which one could select anything one wanted, and the food was free. The area was called The Delta Sky Club. We sampled foods popular in varied cultures and then enjoyed dessert, a combination of ice cream and pudding. Everything was delicious, from appetizers to that tasty treat at the close of the meal.

Next came going into the arena. The room was huge and with a capacity of 20,789. In the center of the basketball court toward the ceiling was a four-sided Jumbotron. The court and each section of the audience could be seen on it.

We went to our seats in the second row and noted that the first row, but not directly in front of us, had three men with high-tech cameras. They were taking single shots and making videos of portions of the soon-to-be basketball game. Shortly after being seated, my wife gasped as the NY Knicks came onto the court. "I've never seen such tall men in my life," she exclaimed. I agreed with her as the game began.

It was about a half-hour into the game when the Knicks got a "free throw." The player Carmelo Anthony stood in front of the hoop and threw the ball, which hit the rim and bounced off it into the air. Where it landed was a puzzlement and the normally cheering and talking crowd became silent. "Where was the ball?" I wondered. Then, looking to my left to ask my wife if she saw where the ball went, I noticed her holding it. Her arms were wrapped around it as if it needed protection. Our son leaned forward and told his mom to release the ball and throw it back onto the court. She replied, "No, I'm going to keep it and get the players to sign it at half time and then give it to your nephews as a trophy." Our son was momentarily silent, I was silent, and so was everyone in the arena. All were looking for the ball. The Jumbotron scanned the room.

Carmelo Anthony stepped out onto the court to look around, as our son pleaded with his mom to return the ball. He explained that she couldn't keep it and had to return it to the court. But she would not hear of such a thing, proclaiming yet again that she was going to get the Knicks' players to sign the ball and then give it to her grandsons. Ah, what should we do with such stubbornness? Our son was texting everyone he knew to say his mom had the ball. He told her to return the ball, and I reiterated his instruction. Our daughter-in-law was silent.

Chapter 16

The arena was still totally hushed when Carmelo saw my wife's arms wrapped around his team's basketball that'd hit the rim. He came forward, and as she explained it, he gave her a backward wave. The Jumbotron was now fixed on her and her every movement. Actually, Carmelo's gesture was to, "Give me back the ball!" She responded by removing one hand from the basketball and giving him, " . . . a frontward wave."

Carmelo then took both his hands and gestured for her to return the ball. The arena was still silent, as she realized that if she returned this double backward wave, with a double hand frontwards wave that the ball would fall from her lap onto the floor. It would probably roll forward under the seats and he'd run toward her to get it.

So, with our voices in unison, my son and I told her to throw the ball back to Carmelo or he'd come to get it. In fact, he took a step forward, and, when he did, she threw the ball to him and he caught it. Twenty-plus thousand people burst into applause and cheered. My wife, when telling friends and family about this experience, explained that of all the presentations she'd ever given here and abroad, she'd never received such an ovation! This was clearly her fifteen seconds of fame!

Most frequently, when others hear this story, they laugh. Before the game was over, my wife went to the Ladies' Room and a security guard along the way stopped her and asked her what she thought she was doing by holding onto the basketball. She explained her intentions and he countered with how keeping the caught ball and getting it signed was done in baseball and not basketball. She admitted she knew nothing about the basketball game but had learned quickly. Pointing to the double rack of basketballs in her line of vision, she questioned "You have so many extra basketballs; what would my keeping one of them matter?" The security guard shrugged his shoulders and turned away, ignoring her question.

When the game ended, some people, recognizing her from the Jumbotron, just shook their heads in disbelief that she intended to keep the basketball. When people hear this story, the response is most frequently, laughter. But my wife was beaming at the thought of how holding onto a basketball and returning it caused 20,000 people to cheer and applaud. All in all, we let her bask in her glory and recognition of her returning the basketball.

Activity for this story: Review the forms of the plot from chapter 5 and create a video with characters and the components of the plot. Work in groups if necessary to create a mini-play for classroom viewing. This activity could then be carried over to other classrooms in a showing of the video or actual performance of it. Of course, a script would need to be written and the video play would need actors and directors.

APPENDICES

APPENDIX A: AUTHOR'S CLOSING THOUGHTS

APPENDIX B: AUTHOR'S POETRY ABOUT TEACHING

Appendix A
Author's Closing Thoughts

REFLECTIONS

Having taught for many decades, there are things this author came to discover to be important when embracing the teaching profession. Personally, I love what I do. What follows are a few ideas that have and still do impact my teaching and being a human being. I refer to these next numbered statements as "life rules" or "ideas" to live by. Many of them involve social-emotional learning.

Number One: Being kind to students is of utmost importance. These students, regardless of their age or grade level, are their parents' most precious gifts.

Number Two: A person/student is open to learning when in an environment that lets them know their being successful in academics is doable and the mainstay for the classroom.

Number Three: If the subject matter appears too difficult for a student, then adapt the lesson to that student's ability level. Accomplishment allows students to believe in themselves.

Number Four: No matter what subject matter you teach, each one has reading in it, so knowing the components of reading is vital. These are presented in this book's first six chapters.

Number Five: Model being a person of good character so students may copy that behavior. Some character traits worth modeling includes one's being respectful, fair, responsible, kind/caring, showing good citizenship, and being trustworthy (unless someone threatens to take their life or that of others. Or, if you know of child abuse. These cannot be kept a secret but need reporting).

Number Six: Live the statement, "No put downs . . . Only lift ups!" If someone shows poor behavior and makes a negative statement to you about you or another, it doesn't mean you have to copy that behavior.

Number Seven: How you conduct yourself is an act of your conscious will.

Number Eight: You can only give to another that which you first have for yourself. If you have self-respect, you're able to give respect to others. You can only give what you have.

Number Nine: Failure stops you or anyone from one's first success. If you have one you can have as many after that as you choose. But you need the first one to get started.

Number Ten: Thinking and feeling are reciprocal and not necessarily developmental. You can think and feel without being able to verbally express that. A child at any age may use the meta-cognitive skills of evaluating, making an advanced decision, analyzing a situation, and displaying cognition through their actions.

Number Eleven: Be sensitive to the needs of students, they are not all the same—academically or emotionally. We do not learn the same thing the same way at the same time. Learning and teaching are best addressed with comprehension of students' preference when it comes to classroom space, modalities, and processing style.

Number Twelve: Student engagement in learning is very important. Have lessons that are interactive and experientially composed.

Number Thirteen: Go into every situation modeling and teaching the idea of "What may I give to this situation, teaching lesson, or circumstance."

Number Fourteen: I am, and you are "enough" as you are. Appreciate yourself by praising yourself and compliment your students too.

Number Fifteen: There's no harm in feeling good. Find something positive to say each day to yourself and each student in the classroom. Words of encouragement are destiny shapers.

Appendix B
Author's Poetry about Teaching

THE CHILD THAT DREAMS

(Schiering, © 1965)

I am still the child.
And I shall spend these years
dreaming
of what I have not
but wish for and could be.
And you shall teach me.
So that I may grow with
Truth and knowledge
To become the person within my being
Who will turn one day to teach another.
Who is still the child that dreams.

ON TEACHING FIRST GRADE

(Schiering, 1974/'98)

I am searching these questioning faces each day,
These not yet awakened womb-like sleepers.
How do I show them the joy of learning?
I impart a fact here and there or give an answer to queries.
Their hearts are now full of the excitement of discovery.
The pervasive awareness . . . I know . . . I can achieve!
This is a time when sunlight hits the mind.
Its rays spreading forth to every fiber of their being.
Going from the winter of their thoughts to spring and summer.
They are: Awake . . . Alive . . . Ready to learn.
But I am searching for:
What will bring this achievement?
What catalysts will rouse their dormancy,
within our shared environment?
What will enrich each one . . .
Beyond my dreams for them?

A STORY ABOUT YOU AND ME: TEACHER AND LEARNER

(Schiering, 2007)

I shall tell you a story about you and me.
That commences with knowing that
I am who I am, NOW, and
You are who you are, because of your own
experiential pasts!

We are titled teacher and learner.
And these are interchangeable.

The beginning of this story is that
We are all those things we remember.

The middle of the story is what you teach and what I learn.
We require mutual understanding.
in order for anything to have meaning,
There's reliance on what we have lived before our meeting,
And/or
What's presently of interest
And/or
Your way of teaching,
And/or
Causing what's important to you to seem important for me . . .
In this place called school.

It is because these things have relevance
That often I am teaching my-self.
I suppose this is also true for you.

I believe that what is ultimately learned
Prepares us for being more of *who* we are,
Or
Changing us
Or
Adding to the "now being" of us.
That's called you and me: teacher and learner.

DEFINING REASON

(Schiering, 2014)

We had a thought, the three of us
Concerning the definition of "reason."
One conveyed it as being logical thought with good sense.
Another said, "Thinking coherently explains it."
The third said that it meant to make assumptions,
infer, and draw conclusions from what had been experienced.
Together we realized we were each correct.
And then we questioned one's being logical, having good sense, and
drawing conclusions.
Each definition brought a new or different
thought, idea, opinion, judgment,
as our feelings impacted our comments, and the
discussion continued. We dissected
these words and tried to reach consensus.
We reasonably regarded reason and reasoning.

A QUESTION

(Schiering, 2007)

Borne from a thought
On a day of rumination
In solitude amidst a crowd
There emerged, within myself,
A pervading question.
It tickled the cortex of this brain and then . . .
It spread slowly to block any extraneous interferences.
This question grew with an insistence and intensity,
and could not be ignored.
The question was:
Who am I as a learner and teacher?

WHO ARE WE?

(M. Schiering, 2007; © 2020)

How do you define me, and how do I define you, or myself?
"I am/ you are . . . a conglomeration of matter that thinks and feels."
Simplistically, that is what some would say.
But I believe that I am more than that, and so are you.
I am as individualistic as they come.
I am centered within a group that does and does not define me.
While there are similarities in size, shape and color ~
There are differences in thoughts, ideas, opinions, judgments, and feelings.
To know "who" we are is to embrace each with reciprocity and equal passion.
"We know few, we acquaint with many," is what I suppose.
I am the "Cognitive Collective," which includes not just a happenstance of meeting,
or even living or working together.
For the most part, I am in a place where "doing" is appreciated.
And so, I write to be among the doing . . . just as you do
your "thing," and we get defined that way.
However, knowing who I am or you are ~ is realizing the "being" of you and me.
So, you may say, or I may ask, "Who is this person?
And the answer is:
We're the ones that have managed to create a linkage
across an indiscriminate time continuum.
We are those who are in the act of being. It's nothing more or less than that . . .
but, perhaps different from one another . . . and that's a good thing, I imagine.
Why?
Because when we come together, we may share those thoughts
and feelings spoken of earlier . . . and in so doing, create
a community, where we are...you, me, and us.
Joined together as "one" with a singular goal of
A civil society, a truly shared environment exhibiting caring and kindness . . .
for the betterment of humanity.

BEING FOR MYSELF

(Schiering, 1985 and 2007)

If I am for myself, and others see this
Then
There may be an inclination to find out what I know
And others will join with me
In
Teaching and Learning.
But if I am only for myself
Then others may well choose to be separate from me
And
Generally, not interested in realizing
There's much to be shared.
I think that as teachers and learners
We are not alone or only for one's self.
We're in a field that connotes togetherness,
As
Each of us teaches and learns, simultaneously.
We are joined in a profession
That has an indefinite time continuum.
One experience builds upon another.
We are known to be those who
Care, show concern, and are responsible
By
Creating learning experiences that form
One's having positive self-images and esteem.
How?
By actively engaging learners in
Learning and teaching experiences.
If only concerned with what works for me
Being what should work for you
Then we're "separate from" instead of "together with."
So, I am for myself but not only for myself.
Where? Everywhere!
When? Now!
Every day!
For all, for now, for always

DID YOU KNOW?

(Schiering, 1995)

Did you know?
I have been teaching for quite a few years.
And that I am concerned about my students learning?

Did you know?
I am brilliant in the classroom.

Did you know?
That I think about students learning
Even when I'm not in school with them?

Were you aware?
That sometimes I think I am smarter and/or less
Informed than others in my field?
I think that this depends on so much—
Like what teaching methods I use
Or who I am as a teacher and learner.

Did you know?
That I am basically a thoughtful person,
And like the willow tree I can bend?

Did you know?
Over the years I have developed
A comfortable level of tact and patience.

Did you know?
When I left college someone told me
I couldn't count on teaching being an exact science.
I've wondered if the knowledge of that truth
Caused me to, now and then, doubt myself.

Did you know?
I sometimes question if I'm successful
In meeting my students' needs.

Did you know?
I have taken graduate courses,
Post graduate courses, and
Professional Development classes.

Appendix B

Did you know?
I have been evaluated, staff-developed, and work-shopped.
I have been evaluated in each of the aforementioned.
I have been defined as disorganized and creative,
Or, structured and responsible.

Did you know?
This depends on who's doing the assessment.
I have been praised and also have not received recognition
When I thought a pat on the back was deserved.
Not so long ago I looked in the sky
And saw geese heading south.
I wanted to follow them,
And the next morning I didn't feel like teaching

Did you know?
I think I am in control of so much, so little,
So great, so small a task.
And, simultaneously, I think I am in control of nothing.

Did you know?
Someone who is not a colleague, but a person
who matters to me
Said something that upset me the other day.
The person used finesse, but the words hurt.

Did you know?
I didn't think I was as effective in the classroom
On that day and felt disappointed in myself.

Did you know?
The very next afternoon
Two of my students commented on
How they like the different ways I teach.
This meant their being engaged in their learning
And my not just talking at them.

Did you know?
This was acknowledgment from students
About "How" I teach.

Did you know?
This is the meaning of Teaching for me.
My using differentiated instruction.

My using ideas from other educators
To create my own teaching style.

Did you know?
A fellow teacher came into my classroom today
And commented on how she liked the projects that
My students were doing.

Did you know?
She wanted to collaborate on ways to implement
These projects in her teaching.
I had wings . . . I could fly.
I felt good.

Did you know?
I am brilliant in the classroom!
Did you know all these things?
Do you know me?
I am YOU!
I am a teacher!

Bibliography

Abott, J. (1994). *Learning Makes Sense: Recreating Education for a Changing Future*. Education, London. 2000.

After, M. (1953/2011). Advice for My Mom: Conversations on Ways to Behave. Presentations in Rochester NY and Columbus, Ohio Children. In *Teaching and Learning: A Model for Academic and Social Cognition*. Rowman & Littlefield, Lanham, MD.

Aurilla, J., Bruno, D., & Giliberti, A. (2021). *Guided Reading Research Packet/Slide Show, Lesson Plan, Oral Presentation and Brochure*. Molloy University EDU. 5060. Rockville Centre, NY.

Berger, D., & Naralie Simpson-White. (2020). *Readers and Writers Workshop Research: Packet/ PowerPoint, Lesson Plan, Brochure, and Oral Presentation*. EDU. 5060: Integrated ELA and Reading. Molloy University, Rockville Centre, NY.

Bruner, J. (2021). *Bruner's Theory on Learning*. Retrieved from https://en.m.wikipedia.org.

Colonna, C. (2009-present). Self-published curriculum. *The Reading Strategies of Orton - Gillingham: Classroom Teacher Practices*. Glen Rock, NJ.

DiBiase, J. (2023). (Unpublished). *A Character Trait Anecdote: Hero*. Early Childhood Education Conference. Molloy University, Rockville Centre, NY.

Dunn, R. (1996/2015). Home Conversations with Dr. Rita Dunn on Addressing Gifted Learners and Processing Styles. Next In 2015 *Learning and Teaching Creative Cognition: The Interactive Book Report*. Rowman & Littlefield, Lanham, MD.

Dunn R., & Dunn, K. (1978–2008). *Teaching Students Through Their Learning Styles: A Practical Approach*. Prentice Hall, Englewood Cliffs, NY.

Dunn, R., & Blake, K. (2008). *Teaching Every Child to Read*. Rowman and Littlefield, Lanham, MD.

Five Ways to Stop Bullying. (2012). Retrieved from https://youtu.be/vGV5jzPYvmo.

Fisher, D. (2023). (Unpublished). *A Character Trait Anecdote: The Donut Shop*. Rochester, NY.

Fontas, I. C., & Pinnell, G. S. (2020). *The Shared Reading Collection.* A Division of Houghton Mifflin Harcourt: Heinemann, Portsmith, NH.

Gerhart, S. (2022). (Unpublished). *Why Are They Laughing?* OLLI (Osher Lifelong Learning Institute). A Class on Short Story Writing. Yavapai College, Prescott, AZ.

Great Source iWrite/ (2006). *The Six Traits of Effective Writing.* Houghton Mifflin Harcourt. Retrieved from http://greatsource.com/iwrite/students/s_6traits.html.

Gurwitz, A., & Schiering, M. (2022). (Self-published). *Conversations on Social-Emotional Learning.* Rochester, NY.

Gurwitz, A. (2023). (Self-published). *A Character Trait Anecdote: My Fourth-Grade Teacher.* Rochester, NY.

Haugsbakk, G., & Nordvelle, Y. (2007). *Definition of Learning.* European Educational Research Journal. Wiley-Blackwell, Hoboken, NJ.

Hausfather, S. J. (1996). Vygotsky and Schooling: Creating a Social Context for Learning. *Action in Teacher Education,* 18(2), 1–10. http://doi.org/10.1080/01626620.1996.10462828.

Levy, J. (2023). (Self-published). *A Character Trait Anecdote: Summer Camp.* EDU. 5060: Integrated ELA and Reading Molloy University, Rockville Centre, NY.

Lodini, P. K. (2023). (Unpublished). *A Character Trait Anecdote: Kevin's Story. A 9/11 Experience.* Stony Point, NY.

McDavid (2004). Welcome to Reader's Workshop. Retrieved from http://www.ourclassweb.com/sites_for_teachers_readers_workshop.htm.

Meyers, A. (2023). (Unpublished). *A Character Trait Anecdote: Types of Kindness.* Director of Field Education in the Sociology Department. Molloy University. Rockville Centre, NY.

Million, J. (1990–2017; 2020). A Rule for Living Well. Psycho-Social Drama Webinar Presentations. Florida and Ohio. 2017: In *What's Right with you: An interactive Character Development Guide and Preventing School Violence: Guidelines for Teaching Civility and School Harmony.* Rowman & Littlefield, Lanham, MD.

Nauman, S. (2022). (Unpublished). *The Howling Cat and Love.* OLLI (Osher Lifelong Learning Institute). A Class on Short Story Writing. Yavapai College, Prescott, AZ.

Offen, A. (2023). (Unpublished) *A Character Trait Anecdote: Helping Hands.* Rochester, NY.

Putnam, G. (2022). (Unpublished). *LuluBelle.* OLLI (Osher Lifelong Learning Institute) A Class on Short Story Writing. Yavapai College, Prescott, AZ.

Schiering, M. S. (1965; '74; '85; '95; '98; 2007; '14). (Self-published). *Collected Works on Author's Poetry: Thoughts on Teaching.* W. Haverstraw and Stony Point, NY.

——— (1967). *"Be Your Own Person…"* Hubbard Avenue School Fifth Grade Curriculum, Columbus, OH.

——— (1974/2013). *A Comparison of Teacher Made Educational Games and Traditional Reading Methods in Visual Perception, Visual Discrimination, Reading Achievements and Reading Attitudes Among Slow Primary Students* (Published master's thesis). College of New Rochelle. New Rochelle, NY. W. Haverstraw, NY. and Website on Teacher Made Educational Games Videos: http://www.Creativecognition4U.com

——— (1975/1999). (Self-published; Published). Interactive Engagement in Learning for First Graders. Railroad Ave. School. West Haverstraw, NY: Doctoral Dissertation. St. John's University. Queens, NY.

——— (1976/2015). (Self-published). Farley Middle School Grade 6 ELA curriculum in Stony Point, NY. One Life/Classroom Rule. In 2015 *Learning and Teaching Creative Cognition: The Interactive Book Report*. Rowman & Littlefield, Lanham, MD.

——— (1977). *Making Learning Accommodations*. Social Studies Sixth Grade Curriculum. Farley Middle School. Stony Point, NY.

——— (1995/2015). Did You Know? In *Learning and Teaching Creative Cognition: The Interactive Book Report*. Rowman & Littlefield, Lanham MD.

——— (1999/2003–2023). *The Reciprocal Thinking Chart and Hierarchal and Reciprocal Thinking Chart with Definition of Skills and the Cognitive Collective*. In the Effects of Learning-style Instructional Resources on Fifth-grade Suburban Students Metacognition, Attitudes, Achievement. and Ability to Teach themselves + The Reciprocity of Thinking Phases and Skills Chart (EdD dissertation). St. John's University, NY and EDU. 5060 @ Molloy University. Rockville Centre, NY.

——— (1999–present/2011) *Quotes for Daily Living*. Continuing Education Workshops for NYS Teacher Certification: Preventing School Violence. Project SAVE Guidelines. In Preventing School Violence: Guidelines for Teaching Civility and School Harmony. Rowman & Littlefield, Lanham, MD

——— (2001). (Self-published). *Digging for a Fossil: A Bullying Story*. Eng. 1620 Children's Literature Course. Molloy University, Rockville Centre, NY.

——— (2003). *The Cognitive Collective Paradigm*. In Raynor et al. (Eds.), *Bridging Theory and Practice*. ELSIN 8th International European Learning Styles Conference. Hull.

——— (2007/2020). *Who Are We? Decision-Making and Problem-solving*. EDU. 506A: Integrated ELA and Reading, and In Preventing School Violence: Guidelines for Teaching Civility and School Harmony. Rowman & Littlefield. Lanham, MD.

——— (2008/2011). *The "Experience of Being. . Feeling."* Presentations at the University of Oslo. Oslo, Norway. In Teaching and Learning: A Model for Academic and Social Cognition. Rowman & Littlefield, Lanham, MD.

——— (Spring, 2009). *Self-Acceptance and Influences on Teaching and Learning*. Eleventh Annual Summer Institute for Faculty and Staff for the Molloy University Faculty Professional Center, Rockville Centre, NY.

——— (2016). *Differentiation of Instruction: Example: Learners' Interests*. In Teaching Creative and Critical Thinking: An Interactive Workbook. Rowman and Littlefield, Lanham, MD.

——— (2019). *Different Learners = Different Ways: The "How To" of the Interactive Method*. In Achieving Differentiated Learning: Using the Interactive Method Workbook. Rowman and Littlefield, Lanham, MD.

——— (2019). Identifying Feelings and Distinguishing them from Thinking. In Special Needs, Different Abilities: The interactive Method for Teaching and Learning. Rowman & Littlefield, Lanham, MD.

——— (2022). (Self-published) *A Character Trait Anecdote: What's That Sound? and Digging for a Fossil: A Bullying Story* Eng.1620: Short Story. Molloy University, Rockville Centre, NY.

Schiering, M. S. et al. (2011). Types of Differentiation. In *Teaching and Learning: A Model for Academic and Social Cognition*. Rowman & Littlefield, Lanham, MD.
Schiering, M. S., & Bogner, D. (2007/2015/2020). The Definitions of Thoughts, Ideas, Opinions, Judgments and Feelings. In *Teaching and Learning: A Model for Academic and Social Cognition; Learning and Teaching Creative Cognition: The Interactive Book Report; Preventing School Violence: Guidelines for Teaching Civility and School Harmony*. Rowman & Littlefield, Lanham, MD.
Schiering, S. D. (1998/2017/2020). *A Story About Respect*. Presentations at St. John's University Doctoral Candidates on Rules for Daily Living. In: What's Right with You: An Interactive Character Development Guide. In: Preventing School Violence: Guidelines for Teaching Civility and School Harmony. Rowman & Littlefield, Lanham, MD.
Schiering, M. S., Schiering, M. R. (2022). *Conversations on Definition of Community and Unity Equaling "U/You."* Dominican University, Blauvelt, NY.
Schiering, G. (2022). (Self-published). *Keeping the Basketball*. OLLI (Osher Lifelong Learning Institute). A Class on Short Story Writing. Yavapai College, Prescott, AZ.
Schiering, G. (2023). (Unpublished). *A Character Trait Anecdote: Where's the Money?* OLLI (Osher Lifelong Learning Institute). A Class on Short Story Writing. Yavapai College. Prescott, AZ.
Schiering, J. A. (2023). (Unpublished). *The Choice*. Classroom Presentation: Becker Middle School. Las Vegas, NV.
Schiering, J. A. (2014–present). *Eradicating Bullying. Article for Reading and Discussion*. In DASA (Dignity for All Students Act) NYS Teacher Certification Workshops/Molloy University Division of Continuing Education, Rockville Centre, NY.
Schiering, J. (2017). Social-Emotional Learning: Eradicating Bullying. *Modifications on Eradicating Bullying Article*. In What's Right with You. An Interactive Character Development Guide. Rowman & Littlefield, Lanham, MD.
Schiff-After, M. (1953). *You'll Get More with Sugar…Mom's Advice*. Rochester, NY.
Schwartz, K. (1995). *A Patient's Story*. The Boston Globe Magazine, Boston, MA.
Simpson-White, N., & Berger, D. (2020). *Readers and Writers Workshop Research: Packet/PowerPoint, Lesson Plan, Brochure, and Oral Presentation*. EDU. 5060: Integrated ELA and Reading. Molloy University, Rockville Centre, NY.
Thurber, J. (2022). (Unpublished). *The Helmet*. OLLI (Osher Lifelong Learning Institute). A Class on Short Story Writing. Yavapai College. Prescott, AZ.
Victor-Fassman (2023). (Unpublished). *A Character Trait Anecdote: A Graduate Class Instruction*. Molloy University, Rockville Centre, NY.
Vygotsky, L. S. (1978). *Mind in Society*. Harvard University Press, Cambridge, MA. (1986; 2015; 2020). In: Learning and Teaching Creative Cognition: The Interactive Book Report. Zone of Proximal Development. Rowman & Littlefield, Lanham, MD.
Wenger, E. (2006). Communities of Practice: A Brief Introduction. Retrieved from http://ewenger.com/theory/index.htm.
Ziglar, Z. (2020). *Quotes by Ziglar: F.E.A.R. is False Evidence Appearing Real*. Retrieved from https://www.youtube.com. Les Brown, and https://stephenreedministries.com.

Index

Note: Page locators in italics refer to figures.

active engagement component, 107
activity Sheet: directions, 40; questions, 40–41
affirmation statements, 72, 74, 75
anecdotes, 133–34; on character traits, 134; "College Graduate Class", 138–40; "The Donut Shop", 136–37; "Helping Hands", 138; "Hero", 136; "Kevin's Story", 135; "My Fourth Grade Teacher", 134–35; Person of Good Character, 133–46; "Summer Camp", 140–41; "Types of Kindness", 143–44; "What's That Sound?", 141–43; "Where's the Money?", 145–46
Anthony, Carmello, 167, 168
applied comprehension, 25–26, 28, 55; examples of personalizing questions, 27
attention, lesson plans, 20; reading strategy, 66; teacher's attention to student needs, 116
auditory activity, 82

Balanced Literacy (BL): analytical/expository, 124–25; assessment, 127–28; character counts, 128; differentiation of instruction, 128; imaginative/narrative, 124; independent writing benefits, 125–26; independent writing strategy, 123–24; lesson activities, 126–27; lesson plan objectives, 126; motivation, 126; plot diagram, 128; practical/informative, 124; SEL, 128; sensory/descriptive, 124; strategy, 115
"Being for Myself", 179
beliefs, 4, 34, 37; in-class activity, 35–36; pre-activity, 35; teaching, in-class activity, 35. *See also* values
BL. *See* balanced literacy
The Boston Globe Magazine, 139
Bruner, J., 114
Buddy Bullfrog, 24, 26, 72
bullying, 37, 95–100

character, 31, 34; development, xxii, 57–58; and social-emotional learning, 72–74; teaching with SEL, 32–33; traits, 33–34
character counts, 128; balanced literacy, independent writing, 128; guided reading, 120–21; Orton–Gillingham Strategy, 83–84; reader's and writer's workshop, 95; reciprocal reading,

187

72–74; shared reading, 111; with social-emotional learning, 31–43
"The Child That Dreams" (poem), 173
The Choice, 126, 155–58
choral reading, 106
clarifier, 64, 67, 69
classroom; activity, 15–16; activity with getting acquainted, 39–41; community, 31–33, 35, 39–43; environment, 73; rule, 74–75; skills for good character and SEL, 38; smart board, 80, 81, 93, 108, 140; thinking skills in, 9
climatic moment, 29, 30
closed syllable, 78, 80, 82–84
cognitive skill, 8, 90; development, 125
"College Graduate Class", 138–40
commonalities, 34
community, 31, 32, 107. *See also* classroom, community
comprehension, 21, 23–25, 51, 67; applied comprehension, 25–27, 55; contrasting applied understandings, 26–27; implied comprehension, 26, 55–56; literal comprehension, 26, 55; questions, 27–28, 55
conferencing, 87, 92
consonant-le, 78
constructive criticism, 59
constructive sharing, 130

DASA (Dignity for All Students Act), 36
decision-making, 20, 64, 108, 116
decision-making graphic organizer (DMGO), 67, 72, *73*
"Defining Reason" (poem), 176
de-stressing, 27
DiBiase, Julia, 136
"Did You Know?" (poem), 180–82
differentiation: in character development, 57–58; of instruction, 12, 56, 57, 71, 83, 94, 110, 128; social-emotional learning, 57–58; types, 56–57

"Digging for a Fossil: A Bullying Story", 149–52
Dignity for All Students workshops, 48
discussion-style method, 63
disrespect. *See* bullying
DMGO. *See* decision-making graphic organizer
"The Donut Shop", 136–37
drafting, 88
"Driving the Truth Home", 158–60
Dunn, R., xx
dyslexia, 77

early reader, 113
echo reading, 106
Edison, Thomas, 95
editing, 88
emergent reader, 113
emotional competence, 33–34
eradicate, 97–98
Eradicating Bullying (Schiering, J.), 95
evaluating, 7, 28, 88
excited mood, 19
"The Experience of Being," 13
exposition, 29, 30

falling action, 29, 30, 69
feelings, 9, 10, 16, 17, 144; definition, 13; feeling words, 14; myriad of, 13; *versus* thinking, 14; *versus* thoughts, 14–15
final decision, 72
finger spelling, 79, 83
"First Bicycle Ride", 18–19, 30
Fisher, David, 136
Flash cards, 80, 81
Flip-chute, 71
fluent reader, 113–14
follow-up activities, 40, 42, 74
Fountas, Irene C., 111

Gerhart, Susan, 162
"Getting Acquainted," 34
Gillingham, Anna, 77, 78
Gillingham Manual, 78

Glean affirmation statements, 74
GR. *See* guided reading
group selection, 71
group work, 70, 107, 128
Guided Reading (GR): activities, 119–20; benefits, 114–15; character counts, 120–21; components, 116–17; differentiation of instruction, 120; early reader, 113; emergent reader, 113; fluent reader, 113–14; key elements, 114; KWL chart, 121; lesson objectives, 116–17; levels, 117–19; SEL, 120–21; stories, 117; strategy, 113; teacher's role in, 114; textbooks, 116
guided writing, 88
Gurwitz, Alan, 134

Hausfather, S. J., 32
"The Helmet: A Time Travel Tale", 153–55
"Helping Hands", 138
hemispheric dominance, 66
"Hero", 136
Hierarchical thinking, 4, 9, 64; phases, 6, 6–7
"The Howling Cat and Love", 117, 160–62
Hurts on the Heart, an in-class activity, 49, 50

ideas, 5, 36, 38, 48, 49, 58, 64, 69, 91, 104, 171. *See also* thinking; thoughts
implied comprehension, 26, 28, 55–56
inclusive classroom, xxiii, 57
independent reading, 87, 92, 115
independent writing, 89; and balanced literacy. *See* balanced literacy
international character traits, 33
inventing, 7

judgments, 5

"Keeping the Basketball", 167–68
"Kevin's Story", 135

"Kick Cancer Overboard", 137
KWL chart, 121

Learners: advanced learners, 56; English language learners, 67; interests, 56–57, 71; needs, 57
Learning: by ability level, 56; activities, 69–70, 81–83, 126; by pace, 56
left-hemispheric processors, 66
Lesson extension, 57–58
lesson plan, 56, 87, 116; balanced literacy, independent writing, 126; contents, 54–55, 57; for grades 1-4, 67–68; Orton-Gillingham, 80; purpose, 53–54; reader's and writer's workshop, 91; reciprocal reading, 67–70; shared reading, 108
leveled reading, 113, 116, 118
Levy, Jake, 140
Likert scale, 110
literal comprehension, 25, 55
literature, 67, 86–87
Lodini, P. K., 135
LuluBelle, 164–66

memory: example, 18–19; questions for use of, 20–21; requirement, 17–18; review involving memory application, 19; story, types, 20
metacognitive processes, 9, 108
Meyers, Amy, 143
mid-workshop teaching, 89
Mini Lesson: in Reader's Workshop, 87–89, 91–92; in Writer's Workshop, 88, 92
model behaviors, xxi
Molloy University, 36, 48
motivation: balanced literacy, 126; independent writing, 127; Orton–Gillingham Strategy, 81; reader's and writer's workshop, 91; reciprocal reading, 68; shared reading, 103; techniques, 54, 71
multi-modality approach, 54, 80
"My Fourth Grade Teacher", 134–35

Nauman, Sue, 116, 160
New York State, 151
1978 suggestion, 32
1978 Zone of Proximal Development, 114
No put downs...Only lift ups, 74
NY Knicks, 167
N.Y.S. workshops, 36

Offen, Alan, 138
"One Life/Classroom Rule" (Marjorie Schiering), (poem), 74
"On Teaching First Grade," (poem), 174
open syllable, 78
opinion, definition, 5
oral reading, 47–48, 83, 106; evaluation criteria, 50–52; examples, 48–50
orientation, 20
Orton, Samuel T., 77
Orton-Gillingham: activities, 81–83; assessment, 83–84; benefits, 79–80; differentiation, 83; learning objective, 80–81; lesson extension, 83; lesson plan, 80; motivation, 81; oral reading, 83; read sentences, 83; reiteration, 84; spelling words, 83; strategy, 77; student involvement, 80–84; teaching sounds, 78–79
Osher Lifelong Learning Institute (OLLI), 147

"A Patient's Story", 139
phonemic awareness activity, 82–83
Pinnell, Gay Su, 111
plot diagram, 128
plot sequence, 29–30
positive message, 158
positive thinking, 74
predictor, 64, 67, 68
pre-language thinking, 7–9
pre-writing, 88
problem-solving, 20, 116
processing styles, 57
Project SAVE (Safe Schools Against Violence in Education), 36

protector, 91, 93, 95, 152
publishing, 88
Putnam, Gayla, 164

"A Question" (poem), 177
questioner, 64, 67, 68

R-controlled syllable, 78
read-aloud, 104–6
Reader's and Writer's Workshop (R&WW). *See* Reader's Workshop; Writer's Workshop
Reader's Workshop, 86; activities, 92; benefits, 89–91; four components, 87; integration, 92–93; Story Map graphic organizer, 93, *94*; strategy, 85–86. *See also* Writer's Workshop
reading, 17; silent reading, 51; strategies, 53, 54, 60, 66. *See also* guided reading; oral reading; reciprocal reading; shared reading
recalling, 7, 8, 23, 90
Reciprocal Reading (RR): affirmation statements, 75; benefits, 65–66; character counts, 72–74; classroom rule, 74–75; decision-making graphic organizer, 67, 72, *73*; lesson activities with questions, 69–70; lesson plan, 67–68; motivation, 68–69; point of interest, 68; points of interest, 65; reason to use, 66; role cards, 68–69; roles, 64; student involvement, 64–65, 68; social-emotional learning, 72–74; strategy, 63, 67
reciprocal thinking, 4, 9, 64; phases, *6*, 6–7
reciprocity, 4
reflections, 5, 17, 66, 171–72
reflective thinking, 66
resolution, 29, 30
revising, 88
right-hemispheric processors, 65
rising action, 13, 29, 30, 64, 69
risk-taking, 7, 8, 27, 55

Sammy Snail's A Little Time for Quiet, 24–25, 27, 69, 71
Schierin, Joshua, 95
Schiering, G., 145, 167
Schiering, Jolie, 155
Schiering, Marjorie S., 4, 32, 141, 149, 158
Schwartz, Kenneth, 139
SEL. *See* social-emotional learning (SEL)
self-actualizing, 7, 8, 35, 66
self-efficacy, xxiii, 63
shared reading (SR): additional components, 106–7; assessment, 110; benefits, 107–8; character counts, 111; differentiation of instruction, 110; elementary grade, 104; guidelines, 113; lesson directions, 108–10; lesson plan for, 108; objectives, 108–10; read-aloud in, 104–5; SEL, 111; stages, 105–6; strategy, 103–4
sharing, 19, 34, 89, 90, 104, 107
short stories: The Choice, 155–58; Digging for a Fossil: A Bullying Story, 149–52; Driving the Truth Home, 158–60; The Helmet: A Time Travel Tale, 153–55; The Howling Cat and Love, 160–62; Keeping the Basketball, 167–68; LuluBelle, 164–66; Why Are They Laughing?, 162–64
silent reading, 51
singular strategy, 90
Smart Board, 15, 81, 93, 108, 149
social competence, 33
social discourse, 32, 37
social-emotional learning (SEL), xxi–xxiii, 19, 20, 32, 57–58, 72, 74, 83–84, 120–21, 171; balanced literacy, independent writing, 128; beliefs. *See* beliefs; character, 31; classroom activity, 39–43; commonalities, 34; community, 31, 32, 34; emotional competence, 33–34; international character traits, person with good character, 33; modeling examples, 39; in Orton-Gillingham strategy, 83–84; reader's and writer's workshop, 95; reciprocal reading, 72; shared reading, 111; social competence, 33–34; stress, 36–38; teaching classroom skills for good character, 38; teaching good character with, 32–34; teaching social and character skills, 38; values. *See* values
sociocultural theory, 4
spelling words, 83
"A Story About You and Me: Teacher and Learner," (poem), 175
story comprehension, 64, 103
Story Map Graphic Organizer, 92, 93, *94*
story sequencing, 29
stress, 27, 36–38
students, 19, 33, 56, 64, 69–72, 80–84, 89, 105, 106; activities for, 81–83; ADHD student, 65; assignment changing to, 59–60; evaluation, 58–59; GR strategy, 115; nursing student, 139, 140; Orton–Gillingham approach, 79; realize themes, 125; reciprocal reading, 64; on skill development, 86; student-to-student interaction, 128; workshop, 88
summarizer, 64, 67, 69
"Summer Camp", 140–41
syllable, 78. *See also* closed syllable; R-controlled syllable
synthesizing, 7, 38, 90

task cards, 57, 58, 70
teacher, 5, 19, 24, 65, 68, 81, 85, 87, 104–8; evaluations, 58–59; in motivation section, 126; role in GR, 114; teacher-made Tally Sheet, 110; teacher–student engagement, 87

teaching sounds, 78–79
thinking, 3–5, 10, 16; in classroom, 9; *versus* feelings, 14; hierarchical thinking phases, *6*, 6–7; hierarchy of, 4; pre-language thinking, 7–9; reciprocal thinking phases, *6*, 6–7; reciprocity of, 4; teaching of, 5–7; types, 5
thoughts, 5; *versus* feelings, 14–15
Thurber, Jerry, 153
tier lessons, 57
types of kindness, 143–44

understanding. *See* comprehension
UN drawings, 134
"Use of Positive Reward Systems," 101

values, 34, 37; in-class activity, 35–36; pre-activity, 35; teaching about, 35. *See also* beliefs
Victor-Fassman, JoAnn, 138–40

visual activity, 82
vocabulary, 105
Vygotsky, L. S., 4, 32, 114

"What's That Sound?", 141–43
"Where's the Money?", 145–46
"Who Are We?", (Schiering, Marjorie) (poem), 178
"Why Are They Laughing?", 162–64
World Trade Center, New York, 135
Writer's Workshop, 89, 129; activities, 92; benefits, 89–93; lesson objectives, 91–92; lesson plan, 91–93; literature choice, 86–87; motivation, 91; procedure to use, 88–89; Story Map graphic organizer, 93, *94*; strategy, 85–88. *See also* Reader's Workshop

zero tolerance policy, 101
Ziglar, Zig, 37

About the Author and Contributors

Marjorie S. Schiering has devoted her career as a classroom teacher and mother of six to creating a safe educational environment where students want to learn. In so doing, she addresses the social and academic components of teaching, focusing on two basic life statements/in-action rules. These imperatives are: (1) "No Put Downs . . . Only Lift UPS!" (1976) and (2) I am enough" (1990). This author believes that these serve as the underpinning for wherever one is present. For her it was when she was a teacher in Ohio, North Carolina, and Rockland County in New York State, as well as post-graduate professor at St. John's University (doctorate alma mater) and then Molloy University (1999–present).

Dr. S., as she prefers to be called, carries her philosophy of education with her: "We are all teachers of something . . . be engaged, physically/emotionally/mentally in the learning and teaching process. This interaction will stimulate interest and profoundly assist in retention of information."

Having heard the statements addressing "you are who you are" and "It is what is," Dr. S. practices teaching the process of discovering how one best learns and realizing that "what it is" . . . is what you decide to do with your personality and demeanor when interacting with others. Determination and persistence have guided her way in the instruction of self-resolve. Subsequently, she teaches and has presented internationally on the topics of (1) liking yourself, (2) finding what's right about you, (3) using one's imagination effectively, (4) recognizing and developing creativity, (5) critically thinking, creating classroom communities of learners, (6) learning how to motivate and inspire the inner you and others, (7) implementing brain-based education with regard to neuroplasticity, (8) adopting innovative approaches to teaching using her student engagement method, and (9) learning through students having interaction/experiential learning in the classroom as an instruction technique. "Engage the learner and yourself in subject matter for its optimum retention."

Aside from international teaching of these aforementioned concepts, Dr. S. has conducted the New York State Preventing School Violence (Project SAVE, 1999–present) and Dignity for All Students Act (DASA, 2013–present) workshops for Molloy University. This has been each workshop, each month. These workshops are mandated for initial teacher certification in New York State.

Along with knowing what it is to be a person of good character, as emphasized in these previously mentioned workshops, she remains a firm believer in knowing what you're thinking, as it's one's thoughts, ideas, opinions, judgments, and feeling that stimulate the way one acts. To that end, Dr. S. developed, in 1999, a Reciprocal Thinking Phases Chart which was seen in this book, for the purpose of developing, through recognition and application, knowing what one is thinking.

Dr. S. is a former first-, third-, fifth-, and sixth-grade classroom teacher, she's a processing-style trainer, speaker, author, member of the Oxford Round Table, and former advisor to Molloy's student Circle K international organization, as well as Molloy's Phi Delta Kappa. She's written three children's books (*Sammy Snail's...A Little Time for Quiet, Whose Eyes Are These*, and *A Lizard with a Gizzard in a Blizzard*) and one song (lyrics and music) that is the text of the last one of these books. She's an interfaith minister and chaplain. And she brought her innovative ways of creative and critical thinking, as well as encouraging use of one's imagination for interactive and experiential learning to students and teacher in the United States, Norway, Belgium, Denmark, Columbia, South America, England, Latvia, Iceland, Ireland, and the Republic of Georgia. She has taught a minimum of 14,000 students during her years as an educator. Of these, 126 were taught to read using the strategies in this book, as well as those that highly provided student engagement.

READING CHAPTER CONTRIBUTORS

Joe Aurilia

Joe Aurilia is an aspiring elementary school teacher with a dual MS in Childhood Education and Special Education from Molloy University. He was a graduate student of Dr. Marjorie Schiering in 2021. In 2018, Joe obtained a BSBA in Finance from Hofstra University and began his professional career as an accountant before transitioning to education. Reflecting on his previous experiences of working with children, he realized he has a passion for teaching and mentorship.

Joe was raised in Long Island, NY, attending public school in the Half Hollow Hills Central School District. He grew up playing many sports, often coached by his father, and hopes to coach golf, baseball, or football for a high school team. Joe enjoys playing golf with his family and friends, serving as a pro bono coach for his parents. He is also a frequent beachgoer and is often found taking long walks or reading a novel by the sea. Even with these interests, teaching still remains his occupational interest.

Daniel Berger

Daniel obtained his bachelor's degree from Binghamton University in philosophy, politics, and law. After a few years of working, he still felt as though he could be doing a little more. He eventually left his job and began working at a before and after school program where he immediately took to helping with the students and any of their classwork. It took him a few months before he knew he was comfortable with taking the next steps.

It was only a matter of time before he enrolled at Molloy and then graduated with a master's in childhood education. He learned a great deal from student teaching. He spent some time at James A. Dever Elementary in a second-grade class, at Roland A. Chatterton Elementary with a third-grade class, and at Birch Elementary in a fifth-grade classroom. These stops gave him valuable experience with different grade levels and allowed him to sharpen his skills as an educator. He specifically enjoyed teaching math and science at Birch. The lessons can be a little bit more detailed, and the students really learn a lot when they are engaged and interested. It can be a nice break from the rest of the coursework and allows the students to explore math and science.

He is currently tutoring and applying for full-time employment as an elementary school educator!"

Catherine Colonna

Catherine is a fourth-grade teacher in Jersey City, New Jersey. She graduated with a BA in Art History from Trinity College. She studied at Orton Gillingham at Fairleigh Dickinson University. She began teaching in 2002 as a Fourth-grade teacher at a private school in Cliffside Park, NJ. After five years of teaching in private schools, she made the move to public school and started her career in Jersey City as a second-grade special education teacher. After many years as a special education teacher, her position changed to general education teacher. She has taught second-grade for most of her career; however, she has also taught first, third, and fourth grades. The years she spent as an inclusion teacher helped her to create lessons that are accessible to all types of learners. She feels teaching her students how to read and encouraging them to be lifelong learners is the greatest gift she can give them.

Danielle Bruno

Danielle Bruno's passion has always been teaching. From a young age she knew that she wanted to contribute to educating our future generations. She has always wanted to make a difference in the lives of children. Her dream of becoming a teacher came to fruition during the 2020 pandemic when she decided to leave her job and pursue her dream of becoming a teacher. She entered her master's program at Molloy University in spring 2020 to become certified as an early childhood educator. She successfully completed her master's degree program in May of 2022. She earned her undergraduate degree in 2012 from St. Joseph's College in child psychology. The road to earning her bachelor's and master's degree was long and hard but she accomplished her goal.

She is currently employed with the Long Beach School District, entering her second year at Lido Elementary. She has also started an enrichment program at her school called Reader's Theater for grades 1–3. Her goal with this program is to help students develop fluency in reading and promote confidence. Reader's Theater involves students orally reading scripts several times then performing those scripts. Her enrichment program has been very rewarding. She has seen struggling students excel and have fun reading. Being an educator is the most rewarding job, and she looks forward to a long career as an educator.

Alessia Giliberti

Alessia Giliberti is an elementary school teacher from Long Island, NY. Her journey in the field of education has been a thrilling expedition. She earned her master's degree in childhood and special education, grades 1 through 6 from Molloy University in 2022. In the summer of 2022, she had the honor of working as a special education teacher in an Applied Behavioral Analysis Extended School Year Program. This experience solidified her true love and passion for the field of education. In the fall of 2022, she received a full-time position as a fifth-grade teacher in North Bellmore School District on Long Island.

One of the greatest joys in being a teacher is the personal connections formed with her students. The joy lies in nurturing passions and fostering an environment where students feel valued and understood. This is social-emotional learning in practice. Her journey as an educator has been one of personal and professional growth, filled with continuous learning. Being in the classroom continues to bring her immense joy and fulfillment. She looks forward to another year of fostering positive relationships with her students, as she eagerly continues her career in North Bellmore, NY, as a kindergarten teacher!

Natalie Simpson-White

Natalie Simpson-White graduated from Molloy University in 2023 with a master's degree in education. She is currently teaching at Metrowest Elementary School in Orlando, Florida. She teaches the fourth grade. During her reading sessions, she has the opportunity to utilize the reading strategies she learned at Molloy. She especially loves the small group reading where students are encouraged to self-correct any mispronounced words. Her future plans include opening a school for underprivileged young persons who have dropped out of the formal educational system.

www.ingramcontent.com/pod-product-compliance
Lightning Source LLC
Chambersburg PA
CBHW030651230426
43665CB00011B/1046